Revenue Statistics in Asian Countries

1990-2014

TRENDS IN INDONESIA, JAPAN, KOREA, MALAYSIA, THE PHILIPPINES AND SINGAPORE

Please cite this publication as:
OECD (2016), *Revenue Statistics in Asian Countries 2016: Trends in Indonesia, Japan, Korea, Malaysia, the Philippines and Singapore*, OECD Publishing, Paris.
http://dx.doi.org/10.1787/9789264266483-en

ISBN 978-92-64-26647-6 (print)
ISBN 978-92-64-26648-3 (PDF)

Corrigenda to OECD publications may be found on line at: *www.oecd.org/about/publishing/corrigenda.htm*.

Foreword

Revenue Statistics in Asian Countries: Trends in Indonesia, Japan, Korea, Malaysia, the Philippines and Singapore is a joint publication by the OECD Centre for Tax Policy and Administration and the OECD Development Centre. It presents detailed, internationally comparable data on tax revenues for six Asian economies, two of which (Japan and Korea) are OECD members. Its approach is based on the well-established methodology of the *OECD Revenue Statistics*, which has become an essential reference source for OECD member countries. Comparisons are also made with the average for OECD economies and with the average for Latin American and Caribbean (LAC) countries.

In this publication, the term "taxes" is confined to compulsory, unrequited payments to general government. As outlined in the Interpretative Guide to the Revenue Statistics, taxes are "unrequited" in the sense that benefits provided by government to taxpayers are not normally in proportion to their payments. The OECD methodology classifies a tax according to its base: income, profits and capital gains (classified under heading 1000), payroll (heading 3000), property (heading 4000), goods and services (heading 5000) and other taxes (heading 6000). Compulsory social security contributions paid to general government are treated as taxes, and are classified under heading 2000. Much greater detail on the tax concept, the classification of taxes and the accrual basis of reporting is set out in the Interpretative Guide in Annex A.

Extending the OECD methodology to Asian countries makes possible comparisons of tax systems on a consistent basis between countries in Asia, Africa, Latin America and the Caribbean, and the OECD.

The report also provides an overview of the main taxation trends in Indonesia, Japan, Korea, Malaysia, the Philippines and Singapore. It examines changes in both the levels and the composition of tax revenues plus the attribution by sub-level of government between 1990 and 2014.

The report also includes a special feature which discusses the development of segmented taxpayer offices in tax administrations in Asia.

Acknowledgements

Revenue Statistics in Asian Countries: Trends in Indonesia, Japan, Korea, Malaysia, the Philippines and Singapore is jointly produced by the Organisation for Economic Co-operation and Development (OECD) Centre for Tax Policy and Administration and the OECD Development Centre in co-operation with the Asian Development Bank. The staff from these two entities with responsibility for producing the publication were: Kensuke Tanaka, Head of Asia Desk and Jingjing Xia, Statistician/Policy Analyst at the OECD Development Centre under the supervision of Director Mario Pezzini; Michelle Harding, Head, Tax Data and Statistical Analysis, Maurice Nettley, Special Advisor, Emmanuelle Modica, Statistician/Analyst and Osamu Yoshida, Deputy Head, Global Relations of the OECD of the OECD Centre for Tax Policy and Administration under the supervision of the Director Pascal Saint-Amans, Deputy Director Grace Perez-Navarro and the Head of the Tax Policy and Tax Statistics Division David Bradbury. The special feature benefited from useful inputs from the Asian Development Bank, provided by Donghyun Park, Principal Economist and Yuji Miyaki, Public Management Specialist.

The authors would like to thank other staff at the OECD Development Centre and the Centre for Tax Policy and Administration for their invaluable help in completing this publication. Elizabeth Nash from the OECD Development Centre's Communications and Publications team ensured the production of the publication, in both paper and electronic form. Support was also provided by Rintaro Tamaki, Deputy Secretary-General of the OECD as well as Elsa Agustin, Norzalelawati binti Ahmad, Koichoro Aritoshi, Gil Beltran, Rowena Sta Clara, Kenneth Lee, Zhi Wei Lim, Datuk Haji Mohd Esa Abd Manaf, Teresa Mendoza, Rena Nagayama, Hui Li Ng, Kunta Nugraha, Kumara Candra, Ratri Raden, Mohd Shafizan Sapie, Jiehui Shen, Adzhar Sulaiman, Joanne Tan, Mui Choo Teng, Suryani Widarta, Marsidi Zelika. The Centre for Tax Policy and Administration and the Development Centre gratefully acknowledge financial support from the government of Japan. Finally, the authors are also very grateful to colleagues working in national governments with whom they consulted regularly. These institutions include the finance ministries of Indonesia, Malaysia, the Philippines, Singapore, Japan, Korea and the Inland Revenue Board of Malaysia.

Table of contents

LIST OF TABLES

Chapter 1
Tax revenue trends 1990-2014

Chapter 2
Special feature: Large taxpayer services in Asia

Chapter 3
Tax levels and tax structures, 1990-2014

Chapter 4
Country tables, 1997-2014 - Tax revenues

LIST OF FIGURES

Chapter 1
Tax revenue trends, 1990-2014

Chapter 2
Special feature: Large taxpayer services in Asia

Chapter 3
Tax levels and tax structures, 1990-2014

Executive summary

Revenue Statistics in Asian Countries provides internationally comparable data on tax levels and tax structures for six Asian countries: Indonesia, Japan, Korea, Malaysia, the Philippines and Singapore. It also includes a Special Feature, which includes a discussion of the development of segmented taxpayer offices in tax administrations in Asia.

Tax levels in Asian countries, which are defined as the total tax revenue, including social security contributions as a percentage of gross domestic product (GDP), ranged from 12.2% in Indonesia to 32.0% in Japan in 2014. Japan and Korea, the two OECD countries included in the publication, have higher tax-to-GDP ratios (above 24%) than the remaining four countries whose ratios stand below 17%. Ratios in all countries are lower than the OECD average of 34.2% in 2014.

In this publication, "taxes" are defined as compulsory, unrequited payments to general government. Taxes are "unrequited" in the sense that benefits provided by government to taxpayers are not normally in proportion to their payments. The OECD methodology classifies a tax according to its base: income, profits and capital gains, payroll, property, goods and services and other taxes. Compulsory social security contributions (SSCs) paid to general government are classified as taxes. More information on the tax classification and the basis of reporting is set out in the Interpretative Guide in Annex A.

Tax levels in Asian countries in 2014

The Asian economy continues to suffer from the slow recovery of developed countries from the financial crisis, China's economic slowdown, the fall of commodity prices, and some trade protectionist measures. Despite this, Japan, Korea, the Philippines and Singapore experienced increases in their tax-to-GDP ratio between 2013 and 2014, whereas Indonesia and Malaysia experienced decreases. Japan saw the largest increase of 1.7 percentage points due to the increase in value added tax (VAT) revenues over this period following the increase in the VAT rate.

Five of the six Asian countries featured in this publication increased their tax-to-GDP ratios between 2000 and 2014, in part due to tax reforms and the modernisation of their tax systems and administrations. The size of the increases between 2000 and 2014 ranged from 0.9 percentage points in the Philippines to 5.4 percentage points in Japan. The predominant driver of the growth in tax-to-GDP ratios from 2000 to 2014 differed across the five countries. Revenue from taxes on income and profits was the predominant driver of growth in Malaysia and the Philippines, whereas this growth was principally driven by revenues from SSCs in Japan and Korea that increased by over 3.0 percentage points. In Indonesia, the biggest increase occurred in revenues from taxes on goods and services. Singapore experienced a decrease in its tax-to-GDP ratio by 1.6 percentage points over this period mainly due to several decreases in corporate income tax rates.

Tax structures in Asian countries in 2014

The four Southeast Asian countries (Indonesia, Malaysia, the Philippines and Singapore) rely principally on taxes on goods and services and taxes on incomes and profits, which together make up more than 75% of their total tax revenues. In contrast, the tax structures of Japan and Korea are more evenly split between the main categories of tax revenues in 2014, similar to the OECD average.

The share of taxes on incomes and profits as a percentage of taxation has remained relatively steady since 2000 in all countries except Malaysia. Between 2000 and 2014, revenues from these taxes increased by 16 percentage points in Malaysia, mainly driven by corporate income tax revenues (an increase of 14.2 percentage points). In 2014, revenue from taxes on income and profits in Malaysia reached nearly 70% of total taxation whereas this category amounts to between 40 and 45% in the other Southeast Asian countries and between 30 and 35% in Japan, Korea and the OECD on average.

Corporate income taxes are a significant source of tax revenue in all six countries, ranging from 13% as a percentage of total taxation in Korea to around 53% in Malaysia in 2014, compared to the OECD average of 9%. As percentage of GDP, corporate income tax revenues in 2014 were higher than in 2000 in four countries, despite the reduction of corporate income tax rates between 2000 and 2014. As a percentage of total taxation, Indonesia and Singapore – who decreased corporate income tax rates the most significantly during that period – have shown the largest decreases in the share of corporate income tax revenues compared to the early 2000s. In Singapore, the decrease in corporate income tax revenues as a percentage of total taxation in 2014 compared to 2000 was around 11.4 percentage points.

Revenue from taxes on goods and services as a percentage of taxation has evolved differently across the six countries since 2000, remaining relatively steady in four countries and decreasing significantly in Korea (by 8.4 percentage points) and Malaysia (by 15.6 percentage points). Within this category, countries have decreased their reliance on taxes on specific goods and services (mainly excises and import and customs duties) and increased revenues from taxes on general consumption, most notably the VAT. Except for Indonesia, the share of VAT to total tax revenues in 2014 remains smaller than the OECD average of 20% in all other countries included in the publication due to generally lower VAT rates.

Revenues from SSCs are relatively small in Southeast Asian countries, at 2% or less of total revenues in Indonesia and Malaysia and 13% in the Philippines. Singapore does not levy any SSCs. In contrast, SSCs represent around 40% and 27% of total revenue in Japan and Korea respectively compared to 26% in the OECD countries on average.

Tax revenues by level of government

More than 80% of total revenues were collected at the central level of government in the Southeast Asian countries in 2014. In Japan and Korea, revenue collected at the central level stands respectively at 37% and 56% of total revenues. In these two countries, an important part of total revenues are collected by the local governments (23% and 17% respectively) and social security funds (40% and 27% respectively). Tax revenues collected by local government in the Southeast Asian countries range from around 3% in Malaysia (a federal country) to 11% in Indonesia. Singapore, a city-state, has no local government divisions. The corresponding average for OECD unitary countries was 12%.

Special feature findings

Income tax revenues form an important part of tax revenues in Southeast Asian countries and a significant part of these revenues comes from larger taxpayers. The organisational model employed by tax administrators has been evolving in recent years and there has been a clear trend internationally for revenue bodies to organise around different "taxpayer segments" (e.g. large businesses and small businesses). Under this segmented approach, there were a number of reforms in Asian and Pacific countries, focusing on the large taxpayers due to their high tax contributions as well as the often complicated nature of their businesses and related tax affairs. In the Philippines, the Bureau of Internal Revenue (BIR) stepped up monitoring of large taxpayers and took measures to address compliance issues in 2015. In Indonesia the Foreign Enterprise and Individual Tax Office was strengthened to better manage all tax matters relating to foreign-owned firms and individual taxpayers.

CHAPTER 1

TAX REVENUE TRENDS, 1990-2014

1.1. Tax ratios

In light of the United Nation's 2030 Agenda for Sustainable Development, awareness of the need to mobilise government revenue in developing countries to fund public goods and services is increasing. Taxation provides a predictable and sustainable source of government revenue, in contrast with declining development assistance and the volatility of non-tax revenues with respect to commodity prices.

This report presents detailed internationally comparable data on tax revenues of six Asian countries: Indonesia, Japan, Korea, Malaysia, the Philippines and Singapore. This chapter discusses the key tax indicators for this group of countries: the tax-to-GDP ratio, the tax structure and the share of tax revenue by level of government. The discussion supplements the detailed country information found in Chapter 4.

Tax-to-GDP ratios in 2014

The tax-to-GDP ratio is the total tax revenue of a country (including social security contributions) measured as a proportion of the gross domestic product (GDP). In 2014, tax-to-GDP ratios in the six countries included in this publication ranged from 12.2% in Indonesia to 32.0% in Japan. Japan and Korea have relatively high tax-to-GDP ratios (above 24%) compared to Indonesia, Malaysia, the Philippines and Singapore (below 17%), as shown in Figure 1.1. The higher tax-to-GDP ratios in Japan and Korea are partially due to their more diversified economies, which make them more able to collect tax revenue from various economic sectors (Papageorgiou et al, 2015).

Figure 1.1. **Tax-to-GDP ratios (total tax revenue as % of GDP), 2014**

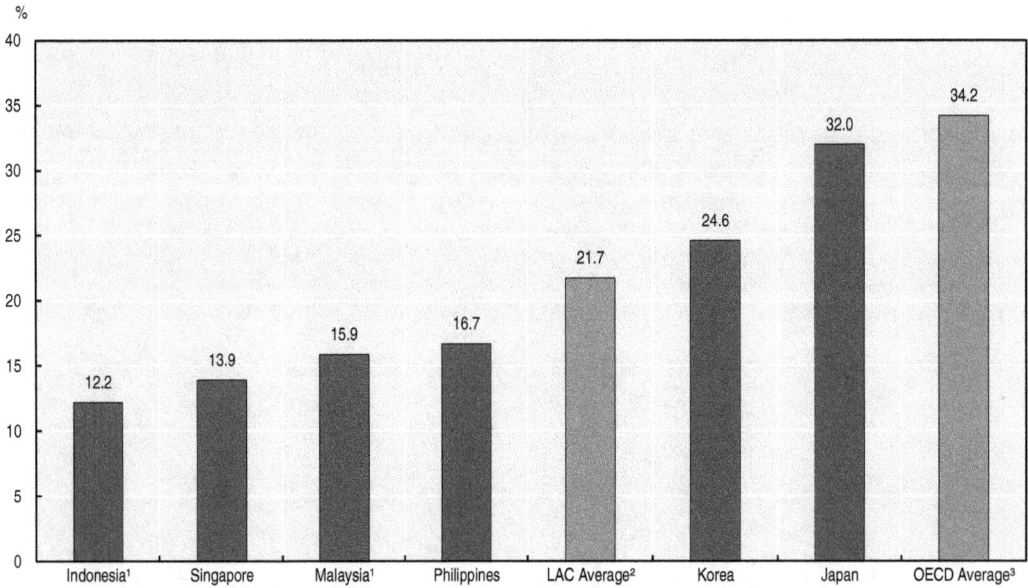

1. The figures exclude state government revenues for Malaysia and social security contributions for Indonesia.
2. Represents the unweighted average for 22 LAC (Latin American and Caribbean) countries.
3. Represents the unweighted average for OECD member countries. Japan and Korea are also part of the OECD (35) group.

Source: Table 3.1.

StatLink http://dx.doi.org/10.1787/888933427792

The tax-to-GDP ratios in Indonesia, Malaysia, the Philippines and Singapore in 2014 were 12.2%, 15.9%, 16.7% and 13.9% of GDP respectively. In the Philippines and Indonesia, the governments are endeavouring to strengthen their tax revenues and have established tax-to-GDP targets. The Philippines aims to increase their tax-to-GDP ratio to 17% (excluding social security contributions) by 2016 (the Philippine Star, 2016) and Indonesia aims to reach the same level by 2019 (OECD, 2015a). These targets will contribute to increasing financial capacity toward the minimum tax-to-GDP ratio of 25% deemed essential to become a developed country (UNESCAP, 2014).

Tax-to-GDP ratios tend to be higher in high-income countries: in general, OECD countries collect a higher amount of tax revenues than non-OECD countries, measured as a percentage of GDP. Asia and Latin American and Caribbean countries have broadly similar income and development levels and similar tax-to-GDP ratios. This is illustrated in Figure 1.2, which shows the tax-to-GDP ratios and GDP per-capita of the six countries of this publication compared with other Asian, Latin American and Caribbean, African and OECD countries.

Singapore has the highest GDP per-capita of the six countries and one of the lowest tax-to-GDP ratios. The high GDP per capita in Singapore results from significant inward flows of foreign direct investment (FDI) due to a highly attractive business climate and a stable political environment (UNCTAD, 2012). The low tax-to-GDP ratio is explained by lower income tax rates (particularly on corporate income) and VAT rates, compared to other Asian countries (UNESCAP, 2014).

Figure 1.2. **Tax-to-GDP ratios and GDP per capita in PPP, 2014**

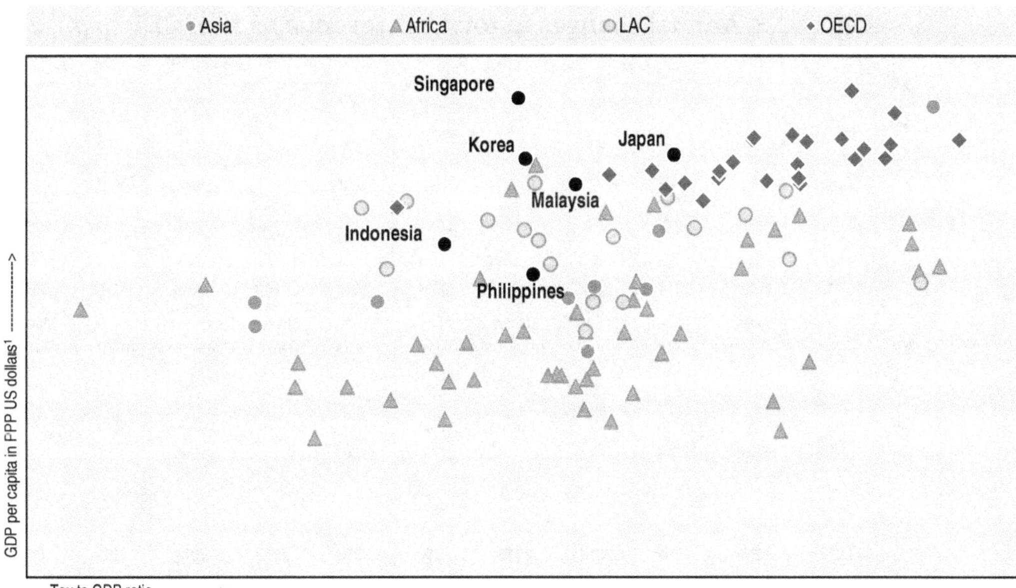

Note: The y-axis is on a logarithmic scale. The tax-to-GDP ratio does not include social security contributions.

1. The Purchasing-power-parity (PPP) between two countries is the rate at which the currency of one country needs to be converted into that of a second country to ensure that a given amount of the first country's currency will purchase the same volume of goods and services in the second country as it does in the first. The implied PPP conversion rate is expressed as national currency per current international dollar. An international dollar has the same purchasing power as the U.S. dollar has in the United States. An international dollar is a hypothetical currency that is used as a means of translating and comparing costs from one country to the other using a common reference point, the US dollar (Definitions derived from IMF, 2016 and WHO, 2015).

Source: IMF (2015), *World Economic Outlook*, October 2015, International Monetary Fund. Tax-to-GDP ratios are sourced from the WEO 2015 to enable comparison across a greater number of countries. Tax-to-GDP ratios (excluding social security contributions) for Korea and Japan are not available in the WEO and are sourced from Table 3.2 of this publication.

StatLink http://dx.doi.org/10.1787/888933427806

In the Southeast Asia region, tax-to-GDP ratios tend to be lower compared to Japan and Korea. This is explained by two main factors: low tax compliance in many countries (UNESCAP, 2016) with the notable exception of Singapore, where tax compliance is high; and narrow tax bases due to numerous tax exemptions and incentives to attract foreign investment (UNESCAP, 2014). In Indonesia, for example, an estimated 44 million people should be paying tax whereas only 27 million are registered and less than 40% of them pay the full amount of income tax (UNESCAP, 2016).

Evolution of tax-to-GDP ratios

The evolution of tax-to-GDP ratios has been different in each country over the last three years. Considering the annual growth of tax-to-GDP ratios, the Philippines and Japan are the only two countries in which the tax-to-GDP ratio grew successively over the last three years. Japan experienced the largest increase between 2013 and 2014 of 1.7 percentage points (p.p.), largely explained by a strong increase in VAT revenue as percentage of GDP. The increase in revenue was principally due to the increase in the VAT rate from 5% to 8% in 2014 (Ernst and Young, 2015).

The other four countries showed differing patterns of tax-to-GDP growth over the same three year period. From 2011 to 2012, all six countries saw increases in their tax-to-GDP ratios; but in 2013, the tax-to-GDP ratio in Korea, Malaysia and Singapore decreased relative to 2012. From 2013 to 2014, Indonesia and Malaysia experienced decreases in their tax-to-GDP ratio in 2014 compared to 2013 whereas the other four countries experienced increases. This is shown on Figure 1.3.

Figure 1.3. **Annual changes in total tax revenue as % of GDP (p.p.), 2012-14**

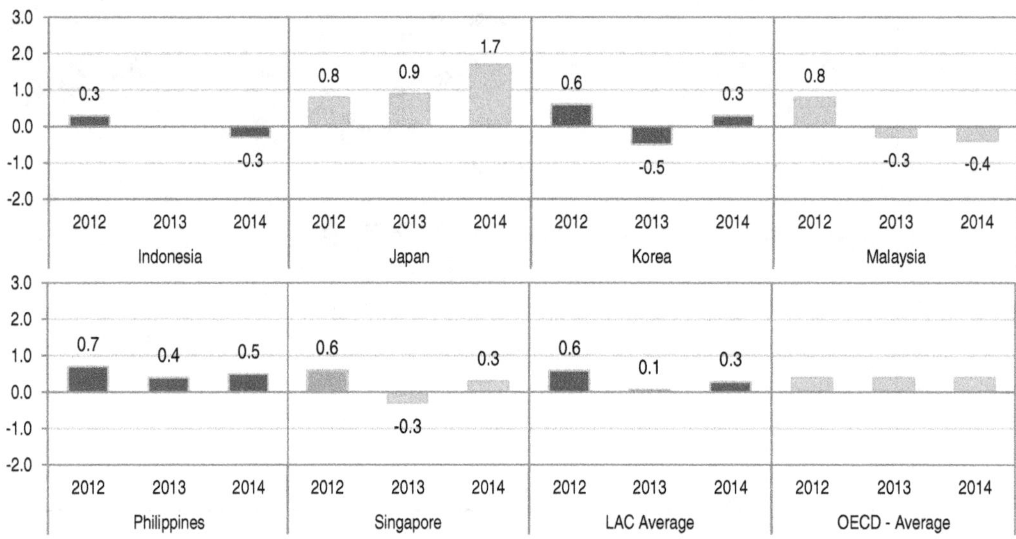

Source: Authors' calculations based on Table 3.1.

StatLink http://dx.doi.org/10.1787/888933427814

The tax-to-GDP ratio is affected by broader macroeconomic conditions. Asia as a whole continues to suffer from the slow recovery of developed countries from the financial crisis, the fall of commodity prices and a number of trade protectionist measures that hinder the rise in exports (UNESCAP, 2014). OECD (2016a) explains that "recent external shocks that are affecting economic activity in the region include (...) China's further economic slowdown". For example, lower international demand for goods and services, reduced commodity prices, and lower investment have slowed GDP growth in Indonesia (OECD, 2015a).

The Asian countries featured in this publication increased their tax-to-GDP ratios between 2000 and 2014, with the exception of Singapore, which decreased by 1.6 p.p. over this period. This is illustrated in Figure 1.4, which shows the tax-to-GDP ratios for the six countries between 1990 and 2014. Since 2003, the rate of growth for the Southeast

Asian countries has been slower than the Latin American and Caribbean countries (LAC) average. Over that period, the LAC average increased by 4.2 p.p. whereas the increase was less than 1.7 p.p. in the Southeast Asian countries. In contrast, the OECD average has increased by 0.2 p.p. since 2000.

Between 2000 and 2014, increases in tax-to-GDP ratios of over 3.0 p.p. occurred in Japan, Korea and Indonesia. In that period Indonesia improved its revenue collection and the efficiency of its tax administration (Arnold, 2012) through the introduction of tax administration reforms in the 2000s, particularly in respect to personal income taxes (OECD, 2015a). One key reform was the creation of offices targeted at specific taxpayer groups such as the high-wealth individual, medium and small taxpayer offices (OECD, 2015b).

Malaysia and the Philippines had increases of 1.3 p.p. and 0.9 p.p., respectively, between 2000 and 2014. The Philippines have modernised their tax administration to increase compliance of certain taxpayer groups (for example, the large taxpayer office was created in 2000) and to improve collection efficiency. In addition major efforts were made to increase the number of taxpayers, resulting in an increase of 71% between 2007 and 2013. However, this has not resulted in significant increase in tax revenues because of limited tax bases and high evasion (OECD, 2015b). In contrast, Singapore's tax-to-GDP ratio decreased by 1.6 p.p. between 2000 and 2014.

Figure 1.4. **Tax-to-GDP ratios, 1990-2014**

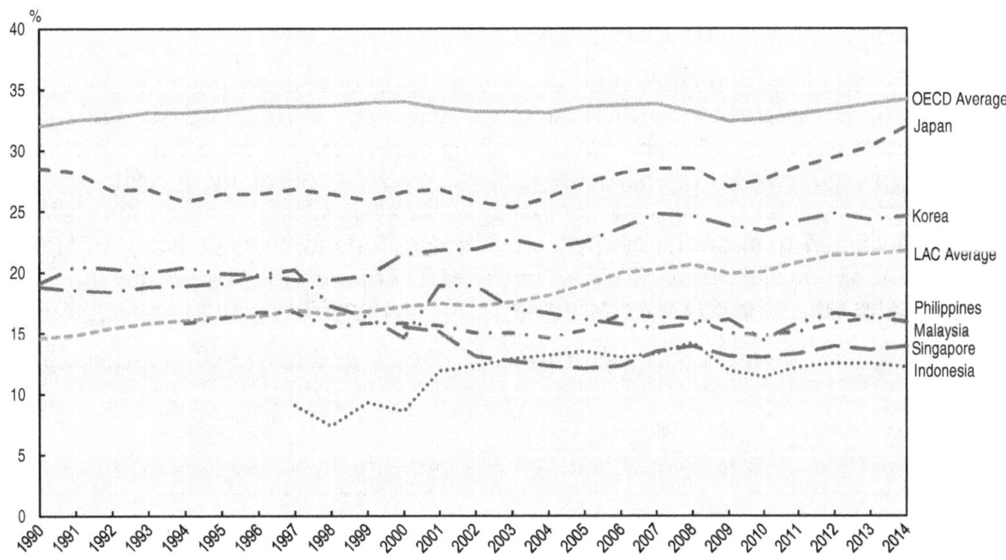

Source: Table 3.1.

StatLink http://dx.doi.org/10.1787/888933427820

The financial crisis affected the tax-to-GDP ratios for the Asian countries featured in this publication. All six countries experienced decreases between 2008 and 2010, ranging from -0.9 p.p. in Singapore and Japan to -2.8 p.p. in Indonesia. Following the crisis, the tax-to-GDP ratios in all countries have increased back toward pre-crisis levels except in Indonesia.

Revenues from each tax category as percentage of GDP decreased in Indonesia, with corporate income tax and VAT revenues most affected over this period. This was due to the impacts of declining GDP growth on tax revenue and the reduction of income tax rates in 2009 as part of a stimulus package that also included the removal of some tax and import duties. Under this package the top personal income tax rate was reduced from 35% to 30% and the corporate income tax rate from 30% to 28% (Basri and Rahardja, 2011).

Factors influencing tax-to-GDP ratios

Tax-to-GDP ratios are influenced by a variety of domestic and international factors. Domestically, macroeconomic characteristics such as the importance of agriculture in the economy, resource endowments, openness to trade and the size of the informal economy can influence tax-to-GDP ratios. The power of tax administrations, the levels of corruption and tax morale (or willingness of people to pay taxes) are also strongly linked to the level of tax revenues (OECD, 2014). Aizenman et al (2015) found that in Asia, government effectiveness and institution quality are positively correlated with the level of tax-to-GDP ratio. Geographic location is also relevant: landlocked countries are less able to impose taxes on goods and services entering the country than island countries (UNESCAP, 2014). In addition, international factors, including the tax policies of other countries, can impact tax-to-GDP ratios.

Higher shares of agriculture in GDP are associated with lower tax-to-GDP ratios (Gupta, 2015; Addison and Levin, 2012; Profeta and Scabrosetti, 2010). This finding is mirrored in the revenue data for most of the Asian countries featured in the publication, where countries with higher shares of agriculture display lower tax-to-GDP ratios. Agriculture amounts to more than 8% of GDP in Indonesia, Malaysia and the Philippines and their tax-to-GDP ratios are all below 17%. In contrast, agriculture is less than 3% of GDP in Japan and Korea and their tax ratios are above 24%. However, in Singapore, the agricultural sector is very small as a share of GDP, but the tax-to-GDP ratio is relatively low.

The inverse relationship between agriculture and tax revenues as a percentage of GDP is explained by several factors. Firstly, agriculture is a challenging sector to tax: most people in this sector in developing economies are on low incomes and many are not registered for tax purposes (EPS PEAKS, 2013). Secondly, agriculture benefits from numerous tax exemptions. For example, Malaysia allows an agriculture allowance to be deducted from profits of eligible businesses (Inland Revenue Board of Malaysia, 2016) and goods and services related to the agriculture sector are exempt from import duty, sales tax and excise duty (Ministry of International Trade and Industry, 2016).

Figure 1.5. **Agriculture as % of GDP and tax-to-GDP ratios, 2014**

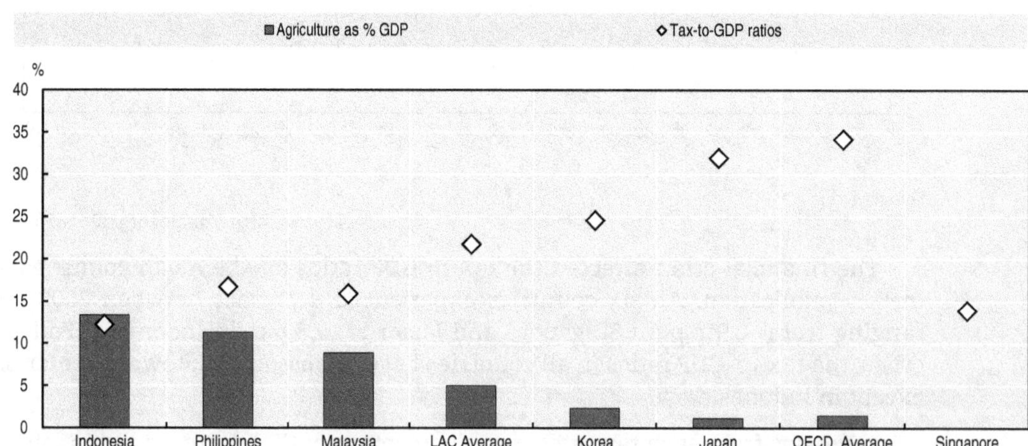

Note: This indicator includes forestry, hunting, and fishing, as well as cultivation of crops and livestock production. The LAC average includes developing Latin American and Caribbean countries only. The average for the OECD countries relates to 2013.

Source: World Bank for the figures on agriculture as percentage of GDP. Table 3.1 for the tax-to-GDP ratios.

StatLink http://dx.doi.org/10.1787/888933427831

Tax exemptions and incentives can reduce the levels of tax ratios. As Southeast Asian countries have increasingly integrated into the global market they have reduced corporate income tax rates and import tariffs, in line with the international trends. The countries have also developed broad tax-incentive schemes to encourage foreign investment. Tax incentive schemes have put pressure on corporate income tax revenues, particularly following ASEAN integration. In 2007, as part of the ASEAN integration, the ASEAN[1] economies endorsed the Economic Community blueprint "to establish ASEAN as a single market and production base making ASEAN more dynamic and competitive with new mechanisms and measures to strengthen the implementation of its existing economic initiatives" (ASEAN, 2008). UNESCAP (2016) explains that "since the adoption of the ASEAN Economic Community blueprint in 2007, several countries have further reduced their CIT rate and expanded tax incentives and exemptions for investors".

Changes in tax-to-GDP ratios from 2000-2014 by tax category

Changes in the overall tax-to-GDP ratios between 2000 and 2014 in the six countries were caused by a variety of changes in the categories of tax revenues. The biggest changes to a category of tax revenue over this period occurred in taxes on incomes and profits as percentage of GDP (where Malaysia showed an increase of 3.2 p.p.) and in social security contributions (where Japan saw an increase of 3.3 p.p.). Changes in each of the subcategories are shown in Figure 1.6.

Figure 1.6. **Changes in tax-to-GDP ratios by type of taxes between 2000 and 2014 (p.p.)**

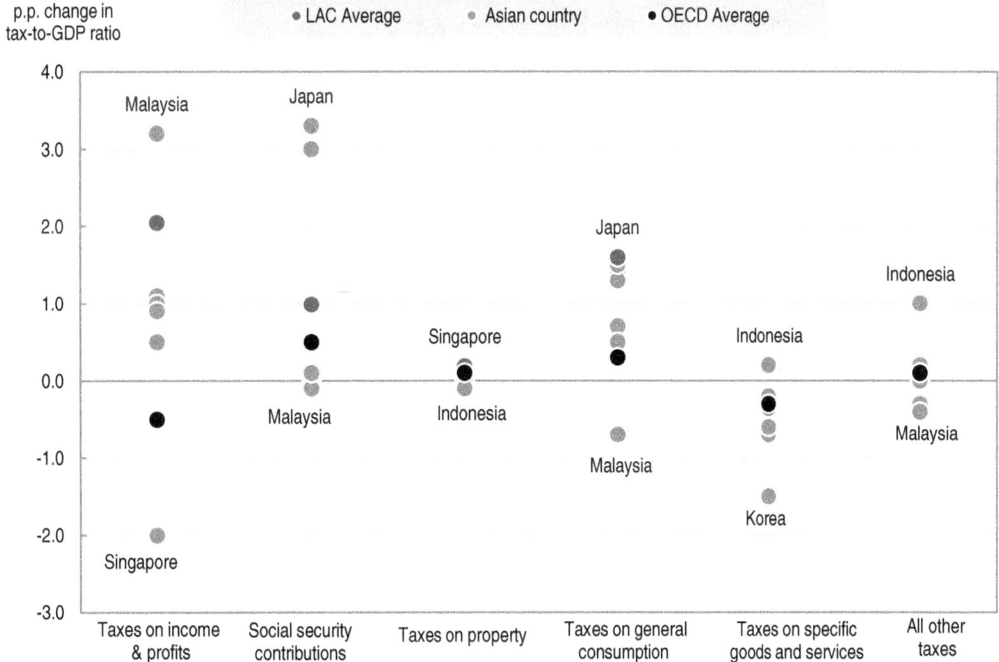

Source: Authors' calculations based on tables in Chapter 3.

StatLink http://dx.doi.org/10.1787/888933427847

In Malaysia and the Philippines, the growth of the tax-to-GDP ratio from 2000 to 2014 is primarily due to increases in taxes on incomes and profits. In Japan and Korea, the predominant driver of growth is the increase in social security contributions whereas in Indonesia, increases were seen across different categories, with the biggest increase in revenues from taxes on goods and services. The tax-to-GDP ratio in Singapore is lower in

2014 relative to 2000, driven by the decrease of individual income tax rates and corporate income tax rates. The change in tax revenues in each category (as a percentage of GDP) between 2000 and 2014 is depicted in Figure 1.7 for each country.

Figure 1.7. **Net changes in tax revenue as % of GDP between 2000 and 2014 by main type of taxes (p.p.)**

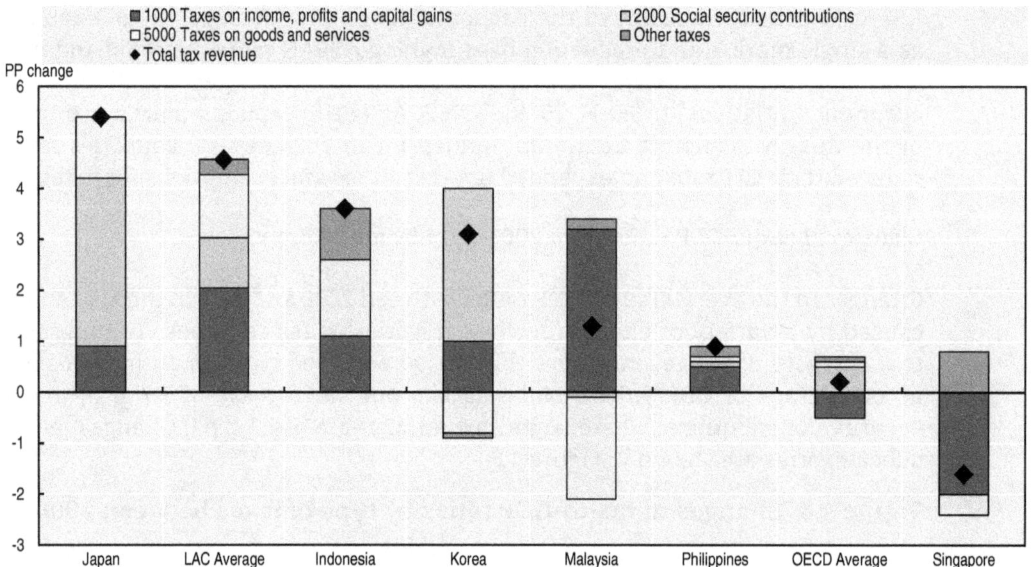

Source: Authors' calculations based on tables in Chapter 3.

StatLink http://dx.doi.org/10.1787/888933427855

The growth of revenue from taxes on incomes and profits as a percentage of GDP in Malaysia and Philippines is consistent with the broader trend for developing countries. As countries increase their level of development they tend to collect more of their tax revenue from taxes on incomes and profits relative to taxes on goods and services (UNESCAP, 2014).

Another contributor to the higher revenues in Malaysia was changes to the tax administration. The most important were providing more autonomy by making the tax administration into a statutory authority in 1996; a change in the tax collection from formal to self-assessment (2000-2004); and deployment of more of the workforce to compliance programs and enforcement tasks. As with many countries both outside and inside the OECD, income tax revenues in Malaysia declined following the financial crisis, by over 1 p.p. in 2010. However the subsequent increase in 2011 returned the tax-to-GDP ratio above the pre-crisis levels. This was partially a reflection of further changes to working practices and the organisation of the tax administration that improved the efficiency of the tax collection process (OECD, 2015b).

In Japan and Korea, social security contributions were the main contributors to the increase in tax revenue as percentage of GDP between 2000 and 2014. The increase in social security contributions in Japan and Korea accounted to more than 3 p.p. of GDP in each country, as shown in Figure 1.7. In Japan, the change resulted from reforms in 2000, 2004 and 2009 to secure the sustainability of social security systems in light of an ageing population. These reforms included increases to premiums and the pensionable age (SSA, 2000; IPSS, 2014).

Japan and Korea have the highest revenues from social security contributions among the six countries as a percentage of GDP. In 2014, social security contributions[2] in

Japan and Korea stood respectively at 12.7% and 6.6% of GDP whereas they represented less than 2.5% of GDP in Indonesia, Malaysia and the Philippines (Figure 1.8). The range of social security contributions as a percentage of GDP reflects the wide divergence of social security systems and the instruments used to deliver social protection in Asia. For example, in Indonesia, social protection takes the form of social assistance (non-contributory) rather that social security system (contributory). Social security contributions are therefore negligible and relate only to the "Asuransi Kesehatan" – a health insurance programme for employees in for-profit state-owned enterprises. In Malaysia, civil servants are not required to contribute to their pensions, which are partially financed from the government budget (Bauer and Thant, 2010).

Figure 1.8. **Tax revenue as % of GDP by main type of taxes, 2014**

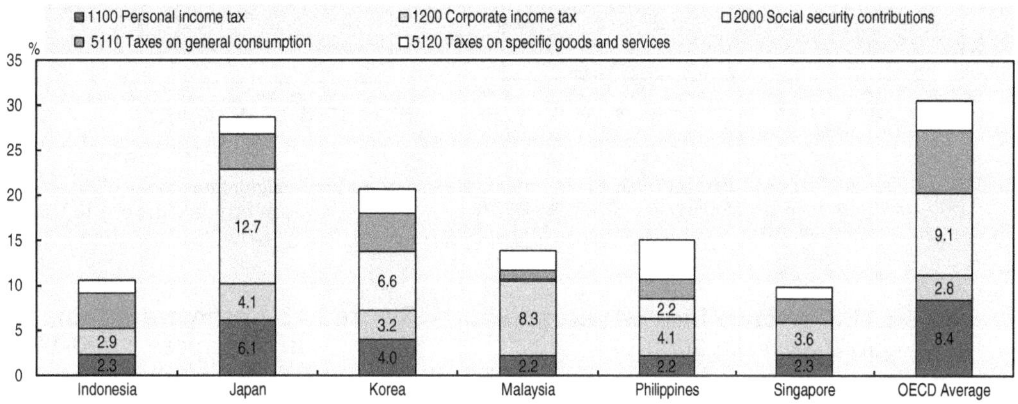

Note: Less than 5% of revenue from taxes on income and profits cannot be allocated to corporate income tax revenue or Personal income tax revenue in Malaysia, the Philippines and Singapore.

Source: Tables in Chapter 3.

StatLink http://dx.doi.org/10.1787/888933427869

Corporate income taxes are a significant source of tax revenue in each of the countries in this publication. The share of corporate income tax revenues-to-GDP is higher in all six countries than the OECD average, ranging from 2.9% of GDP in Indonesia to 8.3% in Malaysia in 2014, compared to the OECD average of 2.8%. Corporate income tax revenue as a percentage of GDP in Malaysia is more than double that of the other countries, which is partly explained by revenue derived from petroleum companies which are taxed at a higher rate (38%) than the standard corporate tax rate (25% in 2014) (Oxford Business Group, 2014). Revenues from petroleum companies represented about 2.4% of GDP in 2014.

Between 2000 and 2014, corporate income tax rates were reduced in each of the six countries, although corporate income tax revenues as percentage of GDP in 2014 remained at the same level or increased compared to 2000, with the exception of Indonesia and Singapore. Corporate income tax revenues in Indonesia began decreasing as a percentage of GDP in 2008, following the first of two decreases in the corporate income tax rate. In Singapore, the fall in corporate income tax revenues as a percentage of GDP coincided with the gradual decline in corporate tax rates from 26% in 2000 to 17% in 2014 (Figure 1.12).

Personal income tax revenues in the six countries are lower as a percentage of GDP than the OECD average. Two factors contribute to these lower levels. Firstly, a larger population of taxpayers are on low incomes and are exempt from paying taxes. Secondly, personal income tax revenue may be reduced by non-compliance and tax evasion of some high income individuals. As a result, in many Asian countries, a small proportion of the population bears the tax burden (UNESCAP, 2014).

Figure 1.9. **Corporate income tax revenue as % of GDP in Indonesia, 2000-14**

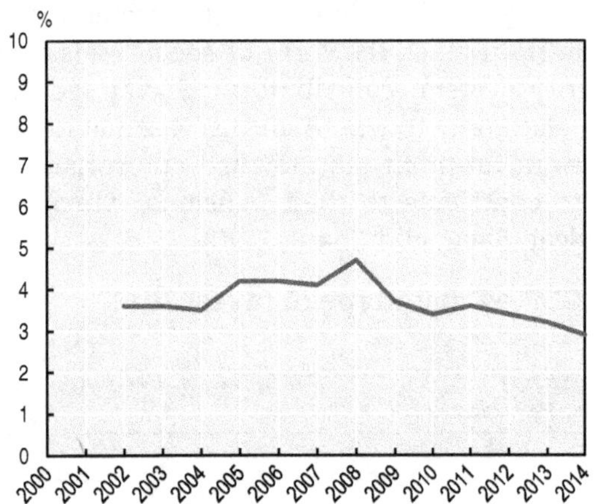

Source: Authors' calculations based on Table 4.1.
StatLink http://dx.doi.org/10.1787/888933427878

Figure 1.10. **Corporate income tax revenue as % of GDP in Singapore, 2000-14**

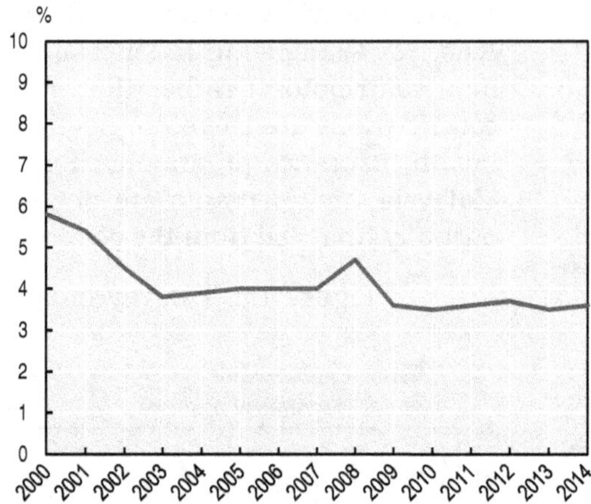

Source: Authors' calculations based on Table 4.5.
StatLink http://dx.doi.org/10.1787/888933427887

Figure 1.11. **Corporate income tax rates in Indonesia, 2000-14**

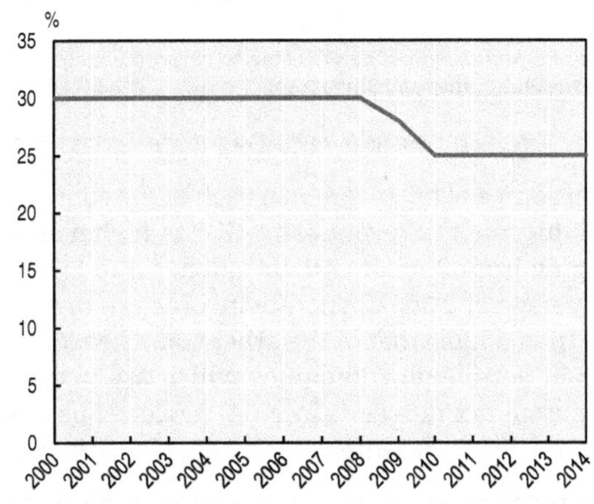

Source: Berlianto (2009) for corporate income tax rates up to 2005, KPMG (2016) for Corporate Income Tax rates for 2006-14.
StatLink http://dx.doi.org/10.1787/888933427895

Figure 1.12. **Corporate income tax rates in Singapore, 2000-14**

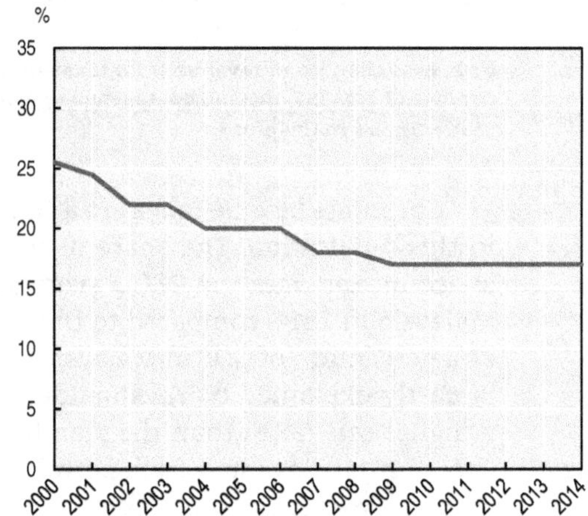

Source: Ministry of Finance of Singapore (MOF).
StatLink http://dx.doi.org/10.1787/888933427904

For example, in Indonesia, 3% of households paid more than 80% of personal tax revenues in 2010 (Nugraha and Lewis, 2011). Higher- and middle-income households in Indonesia may underreport their taxable personal income (Arnold, 2012) and the self-employed are not covered by a withholding system, so it is difficult to assess their taxable income. Indonesia has since taken measures to improve the registration of taxpayers and the number of individual taxpayers has increased from 3.25 million in 2006 to almost 17 million in 2010 (Arnold, 2012).

1.2. Tax structures

The tax structure, measured as the composition of tax revenues of different types, is a second important indicator, since different taxes have different economic and social effects. Across the six countries in this publication, the composition of taxes varies widely, reflecting their different policy choices, economic structures and conditions, tax administration capabilities and historical factors.

Tax structures in 2014 and evolution since 2000

There is a wide divergence of tax structures across the six countries in this publication. The countries can be divided into two main groups:

- The four Southeast Asian countries rely principally on taxes on goods and services and taxes on incomes and profits, which together make up more than 75% of total tax revenue in these countries. Within this group, the share of taxes on incomes and profits and on taxes on goods and services is roughly the same (around 40-45%) in Indonesia, the Philippines and Singapore; whereas revenue from taxes on income and profits in Malaysia generate nearly 70% of total tax revenue.
- In contrast, the tax structures of Japan and Korea are more evenly split between the main categories of tax revenues: in Korea, tax revenue is divided roughly equally into three parts: 29% from taxes on income and profits, 27% from social security contributions, and 30% from taxes on goods and services. This tax structure is similar to the OECD average. In Japan, social security contributions amount to nearly 40% of total tax revenue and the share of taxes on goods and services is slightly below 20%.

Figure 1.13. **Tax structures, 2014**

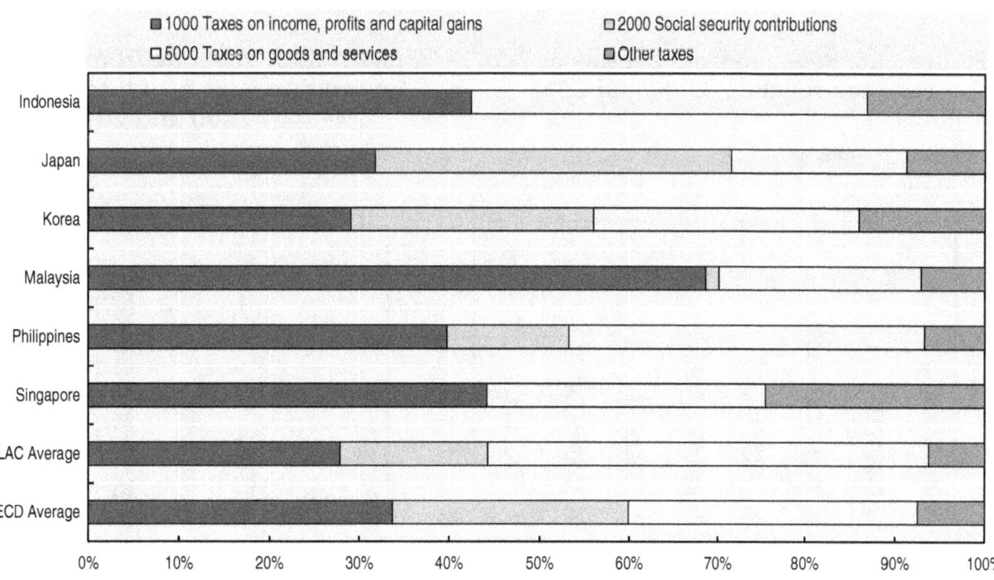

Source: Authors' calculations based on tables in Chapter 4.

StatLink http://dx.doi.org/10.1787/888933427917

Between 2000 and 2014, the Asian countries in this publication decreased their reliance on taxes on specific goods and services (mainly excises and import and customs duties) and increased revenues from taxes on general consumption, most notably VAT (Figure 1.14 and Figure 1.15).

Figure 1.14. **Revenue from taxes on general consumption as % of total tax revenue, 2000 and 2014**

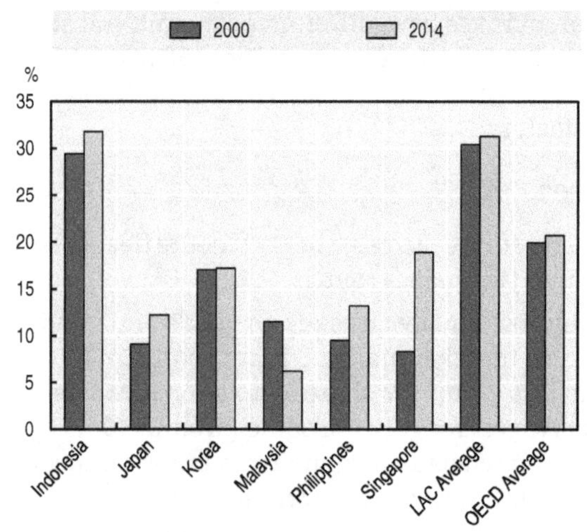

Source: Table 3.13.

StatLink http://dx.doi.org/10.1787/888933427925

Figure 1.15. **Revenue from taxes on specific goods and services as % of total tax revenue, 2000 and 2014**

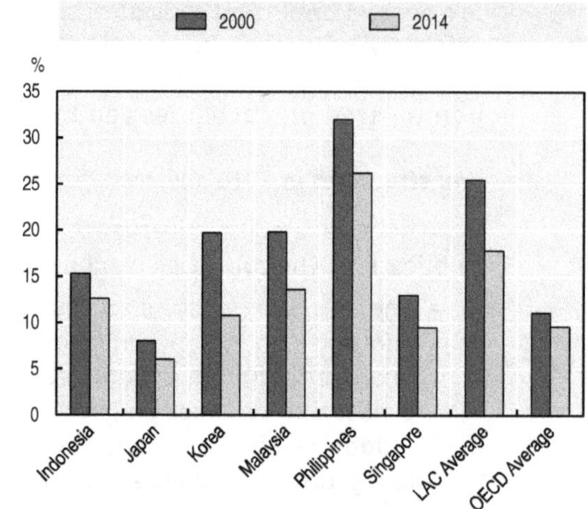

Source: Table 3.15.

StatLink http://dx.doi.org/10.1787/888933427939

Over the past decades, tax revenues from import duties have decreased in many countries, partly due to trade liberalisation that took the form of reductions of tariffs and new trade agreements (UNESCAP, 2014). Since 2000, dozens of bilateral and regional trade agreements have been signed by East Asian countries (Pomfret and Sourdin, 2011). In January 2007, the ASEAN countries agreed that tariffs on all intra-ASEAN goods would be eliminated by 2015 (Safuan, 2012).

Figure 1.16. **Revenue from excises as % of total tax revenue, 2000 and 2014**

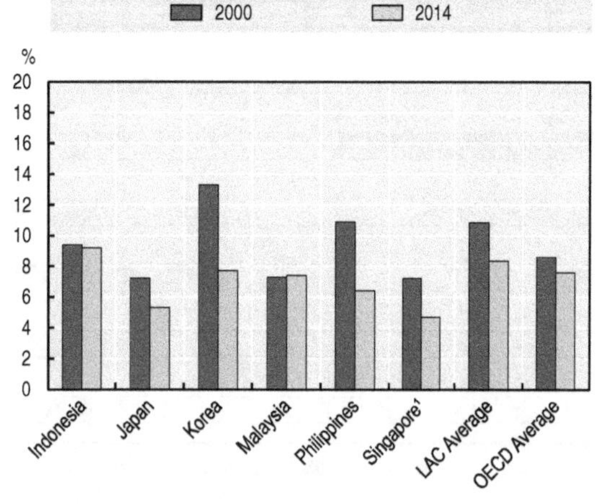

1. Customs and import duties cannot be separated from excises in Singapore and have been classified in category 5121 Excises.

Source: Authors' calculations based on tables in Chapter 4.

StatLink http://dx.doi.org/10.1787/888933427945

Figure 1.17. **Revenue from customs and import duties as % of total tax revenue, 2000 and 2014**

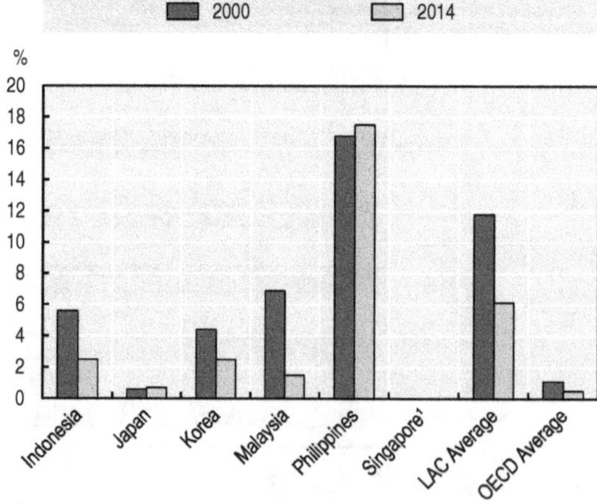

1. Customs and import duties cannot be separated from excises in Singapore and have been classified in category 5121 Excises.

Source: Authors' calculations based on tables in Chapter 4.

StatLink http://dx.doi.org/10.1787/888933427952

The types of taxes levied at local government level vary between countries. Local governments in Malaysia and the Philippines have a narrow range of taxes under their jurisdiction, relying on property taxes (both countries) and taxes on income and profits (the Philippines only). Local governments in Japan and Korea raised revenue from taxes on income and profits, property taxes, taxes on goods and services, payroll (Korea only) and other taxes.

Figure 1.20. **Composition of local government tax revenue by main type of taxes, 2014**

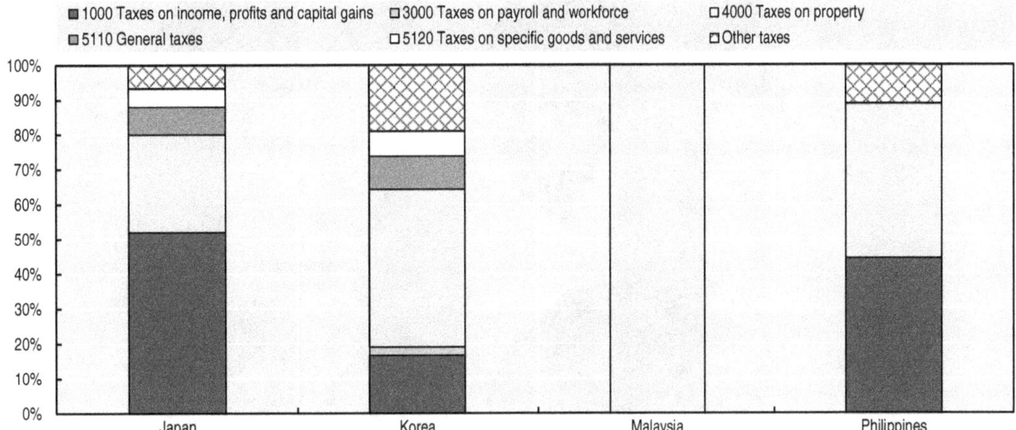

Note: The composition of local tax revenue is unknown for Indonesia and is currently allocated to 6000 Other taxes.

Source: OECD (2016b), "Revenue Statistics in Asia: Comparative tables", *OECD Tax Statistics* (database), http://dx.doi.org/10.1787/eabf71c2-en.

StatLink http://dx.doi.org/10.1787/888933427988

Between 2000 and 2014 the share of revenues collected by local governments in Asian and OECD countries was fairly stable, with the exception of Indonesia in which the share of revenues attributed to local governments increased by 7.2 p.p.

The proportion of total revenues collected by social security funds in Indonesia and Malaysia was almost zero in 2014, whereas in the Philippines it was 13.2%. This compares with 39.7% in Japan, 26.8% in Korea and 24.5% on average in the OECD unitary countries. The share of revenues from social security funds has increased in both Japan (by 4.3 p.p.) and in Korea (10.1 p.p.) since 2000.

1.4. Comparative figures

Figure 1.21. **Tax structures, 2014**

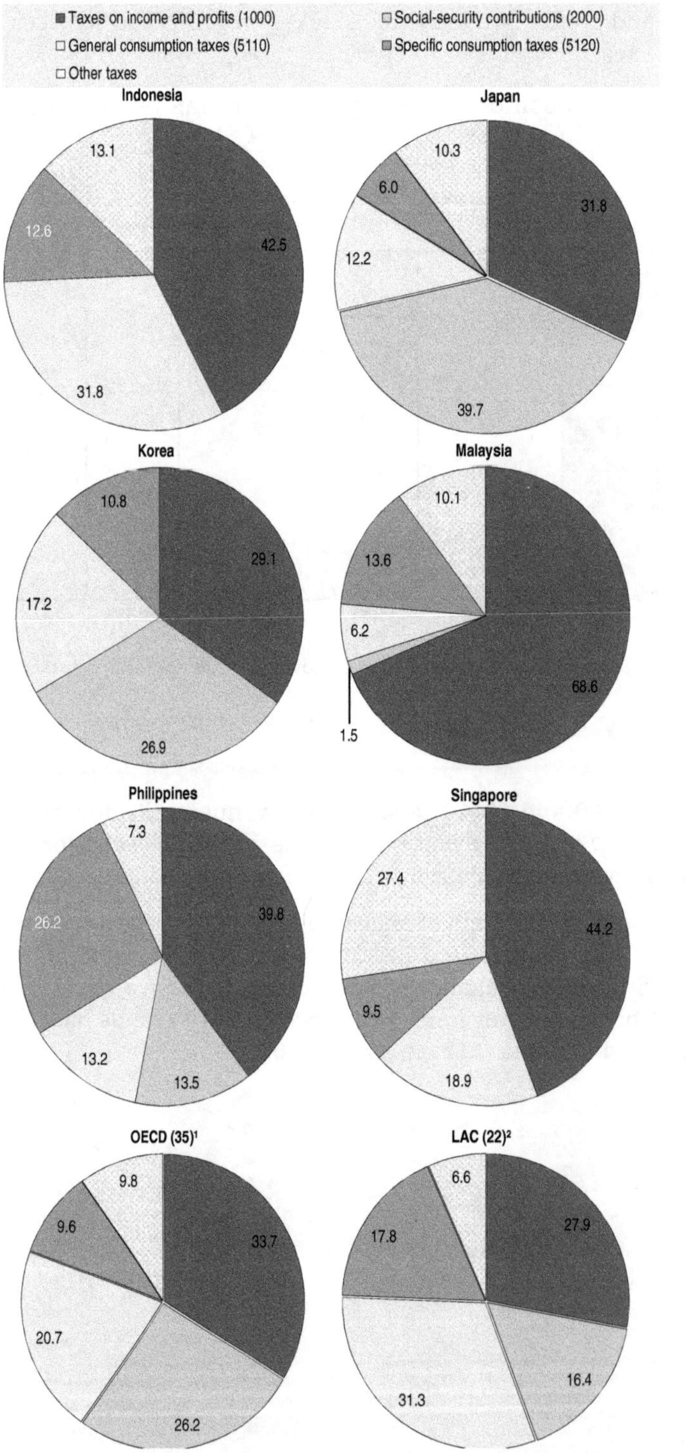

1. Represents the unweighted average for OECD member countries. Japan and Korea are also part of the OECD (35) group.

2. Represents the unweighted average for 22 LAC (Latin American and Caribbean) countries.

Source: Authors' calculations based on tables in Chapter 4.

StatLink http://dx.doi.org/10.1787/888933427999

Notes

1. ASEAN, the Association of Southeast Asian Nations.
2. Singapore does not levy social security contributions.
3. Customs and import duties cannot be separated from excises in Singapore and have been classified in 5111 Excises.

References

Addison, T. and J. Levin (2012), *The Determinants of Tax Revenue in Sub-Saharan Africa*, Swedish Business School at Örebro University, Örebro, Sweden, oru.diva-portal.org/smash/record.jsf?pid=diva2%3A570456&dswid=4207.

Aizenman, et al (2015) "Tax revenue trends in Asia and Latin America: A comparative analysis", *NBER Working Paper*, No. 21755, Cambridge, www.nber.org/papers/w21755.

Arnold, J. (2012), "Improving the Tax System in Indonesia", *OECD Economics Department Working Papers*, No. 998, OECD Publishing, Paris, http://dx.doi.org/10.1787/5k912j3r2qmr-en.

ASEAN (2008), "ASEAN Economic Community Blueprint", The Association of Southeast Asian Nations Secretariat, Jakarta, http://asean.org/wp-content/uploads/archive/5187-10.pdf.

Bauer, A. and M. Thant (2010), *Poverty and Sustainable Development in Asia: Impacts and Responses to the Global Economic Crisis*, ADB Publishing, Mandaluyong City, https://www.adb.org/sites/default/files/publication/27509/poverty-sustainable-development-asia.pdf.

Basri, M.C. and S. Rahardja (2011), "Mild Crisis, Half Hearted Fiscal Stimulus: Indonesia During the GFC", in Ito, T. and F. Parulian (eds.), "Assessment on the Impact of Stimulus, Fiscal Transparency and Fiscal Risk", *ERIA Research Project Report* 2010-01, pp.169-211. ERIA, www.eria.org/publications/research_project_reports/images/pdf/y2010/no1/ch5Basri_and_Rahardja_Indonesia.pdf.

Berlianto, A. (2009), "Tax competition and harmonization in Southeast Asia", Massey University, Albany, New Zealand, http://mro.massey.ac.nz/bitstream/handle/10179/966/02whole.pdf?sequence=1&isAllowed=y.

Bessho, S. (2016), "Case Study of Central and Local Government Finance in Japan", ADBI Working Paper, No 599. Asian Development Bank Institute, Tokyo, https://www.adb.org/publications/case-study-central-and-local-government-finance-japan/.

EPS PEAKS (2013), "Taxation and Developing Countries", Overseas Development Institute training notes, London, https://www.odi.org/sites/odi.org.uk/files/odi-assets/events-documents/5045.pdf.

Ernst and Young (2015), *Indirect taxes in 2015*, EYG no. DL1195, www.ey.com/Publication/vwLUAssets/ey-indirect-tax-developments-in-2015/%24FILE/ey-indirect-tax-developments-in-2015.pdf.

Gupta, P. (2015), "Generating Larger Tax Revenue in South Asia", *MPRA Paper, No. 61443*, https://mpra.ub.uni-muenchen.de/61443/1/MPRA_paper_61443.pdf.

IMF (2016), *World Economic Outlook – Frequently Asked Questions*, https://www.imf.org/external/pubs/ft/weo/faq.htm#q4d.

IMF (2015), *World Economic Outlook: Adjusting to Lower Commodity Prices*, International Monetary Fund, Washington, DC., October.

Inland Revenue Board of Malaysia (2016), "Agriculture allowances public ruling no. 1/2016", www.hasil.gov.my/pdf/pdfam/PR_01_2016.pdf.

IPSS (2014), "Social Security in Japan 2014", National Institute of Population and Social Security Research, Tokyo, www.ipss.go.jp/s-info/e/ssj2014/pdf/SSJ2014.pdf.

KPMG (2016), "Corporate tax rates table", https://home.kpmg.com/xx/en/home/services/tax/tax-tools-and-resources/tax-rates-online/corporate-tax-rates-table.html.

Ministry of International Trade and Industry (2016), Kuala Lumpur, Malaysia, www.miti.gov.my/index.php/pages/view/content5235.html.

Nugraha, K. and P. Lewis (2011), "Market Income, Actual Income and Income Distribution in Indonesia", 40th Australian Conference of Economists paper, Canberra, http://ace2011.org.au/ACE2011/Documents/Abstract_Kunta_Nugraha_Phil_Lewis.pdf.

OECD (2016a), *Economic Outlook for Southeast Asia, China and India 2016: Enhancing Regional Ties*, OECD Publishing, Paris, http://dx.doi.org/10.1787/saeo-2016-en.

OECD (2016b), "Revenue Statistics in Asia: Comparative tables", *OECD Tax Statistics* (database), http://dx.doi.org/10.1787/eabf71c2-en.

OECD, et al. (2016), *Revenue Statistics in Latin America and the Caribbean 2016*, OECD Publishing, Paris, http://dx.doi.org/10.1787/rev_lat_car-2016-en-fr.

OECD (2015a), *OECD Economic Surveys: Indonesia*, OECD Publishing, Paris, http://dx.doi.org/10.1787/eco_surveys-idn-2015-en.

OECD (2015b), *Revenue Statistics in Asian Countries 2015: Trends in Indonesia, Malaysia and the Philippines*, OECD Publishing, Paris, http://dx.doi.org/10.1787/9789264234277-en.

OECD (2014), *Development Co-operation Report 2014: Mobilising Resources for Sustainable Development*, OECD Publishing, Paris, http://dx.doi.org/10.1787/dcr-2014-en.

Oxford Business Group (2014), *The Report: Malaysia 2014*, Oxford Business Group, www.oxfordbusinessgroup.com/malaysia-2014.

Papageorgiou, C. et al (2015), "Diversification, Growth, and Volatility in Asia", *World Bank Policy Research Working Paper*, No 7380, http://documents.worldbank.org/curated/en/271261467986248043/pdf/WPS7380.pdf.

Pomfret, R. and P. Sourdin (2011), "Trade Agreements in Southeast Asia", https://www.wto.org/english/res_e/publications_e/wtr11_forum_e/wtr11_2feb11_e.htm.

Profeta, P. and S. Scabrosetti (2010), *The Political Economy of Taxation: Lessons from Developing Countries*, Edward Elgar Publishing, https://books.google.fr/books?isbn=1849805490.

Safuan, S. (2012), "ASEAN Economic Cooperation: Trade Liberalization Impacts on the National Economy", *International Journal of Economics and Finance*, Vol. 4, No. 11, Canadian Center of Science and Education, http://dx.doi.org/10.5539/ijef.v4n11p66.

SSA (2010), "Public Pension Reform in Japan", *Social Security Bulletin*, Vol. 63, No. 4, https://www.ssa.gov/policy/docs/ssb/v63n4/v63n4p99.pdf.

The Philippine Star (2016), "Despite strong GDP growth Tax collection slows in Q1", www.philstar.com/business/2016/05/21/1585219/despite-strong-gdp-growth-tax-collection-slows-q1.

Tradingeconomics (2016), www.tradingeconomics.com/search.aspx?q=VAT rate.

UNCTAD (2012), *World Investment Report 2012, Towards a new Generation of Investment Policies*, New York and Geneva, http://unctad.org/en/PublicationsLibrary/wir2012_embargoed_en.pdf.

UNESCAP (2016), "Improving tax policy and administration in South-East Asia", *MPFD policy briefs* No. 31, https://www.unescap.org/sites/default/files/MPFD%20Policy%20Briefs%20No.31-SEA.pdf.

UNESCAP (2014), *Economic and Social Survey of Asia and the Pacific 2014, Regional Connectivity for Shared Prosperity*, United Nations, https://www.unescap.org/sites/default/files/Economic%20and%20Social%20Survey%20of%20Asia%20and%20the%20Pacific%202014.pdf.

WHO (2015), "Purchasing Power Parity 2005", www.who.int/choice/costs/ppp/en/.

CHAPTER 2

SPECIAL FEATURE

Large taxpayer services in Asia

Revenues from corporate income taxes play a significant role in total tax revenues in the six countries included in this publication, and are typically higher as a percentage of GDP than in other economies. They ranged from 2.9% of GDP in Indonesia to 8.3% of GDP in Malaysia in 2014, compared to the OECD average of 2.8%. Trends in revenues from corporate income taxes have diverged across Asian countries since 2000. While most of the countries in this publication have increased revenues from corporate income taxes as percentages of GDP compared to the early 2000's, Singapore and Indonesia saw decreases in corporate income tax revenues relative to GDP.

In most countries, corporate income tax revenues are primarily derived from large taxpayers. Large taxpayers often face more complex tax issues and business activities than smaller taxpayers and may also present an additional avoidance risk. Given their significance in the corporate income tax base, it is important that tax administrations are well equipped to monitor and support large taxpayers.

Table 2.1. **Revenue bodies' internal organisation design**

Economy	Selected Units of Internal Organisation Structure (√ where applicable)						
	Structural criteria	Large Taxpayer Division	Dedicated Processing Center	Debt Collection Function	Fraud/ Serious Evasion Function	Dedicated Disputes and Appeals Function	Full In-House Information Technology Function
Brunei Darussalam	F			√			
Cambodia	F	√		√			√
China, P.R.	All	√	√	√	√	√	√
Hong Kong, China	All		√	√	√	√	√
Indonesia	F	√	√	√	√	√	√
Japan	All	√	√	√	√	√	√
Korea, Rep. of	All	*		*	*	√	√
Kyrgyz Republic	F	√		√		√	√
Lao PDR	F	√					
Malaysia	F	√	√	√	√	√	√
Maldives	All	√	√	√	√	√	√
Mongolia	F, TP	√		√		√	√
Myanmar	F						
Papua New Guinea	All			√		√	√
Philippines	All	√	√	√	√	√	√
Singapore	T, F	√**	√	√	√		√
Tajikistan	All	√		√		√	√
Thailand	F, TP	√	√		√	√	√

F=function, T=tax, TP=taxpayer, Lao PDR = Lao People's Democratic Republic
Note: The absence of a tick mark (√) means the feature is "not applicable" as per heading.
* These divisions and units operate only at the regional level.
** There are separate large taxpayer units for both corporate tax and goods and services tax.
Source: ADB (2015) and OECD (2015) survey responses.

There has been a clear trend internationally for revenue bodies to organise around different "taxpayer segments" (e.g. large businesses and small businesses) instead of only focusing on functional groupings, such as taxpayer registration, accounting, debt collection, etc. As elsewhere, large taxpayer services were initially created in the tax administrations of most of the Asian economies. For example, the Philippines created a large taxpayer office in 2000 to increase compliance of this taxpayer group as well as to improve collection efficiency in general.

Organising around taxpayer segments has been strongly encouraged by international organisations over recent decades, particularly for large taxpayers. The rationale for this approach is that each segment of taxpayers has different characteristics and behaviours and, as a result, presents different tax compliance risks that require more tailored treatment. Delivering compliance programmes effectively segment-by-segment is best executed by separate organisational divisions, with their own administrative and risk management approaches. The vast majority of revenue bodies in the 21 economies surveyed reported having a structure based largely along functional lines, and over 75% of them also reported having a dedicated large taxpayer division.

Organisational structures among revenue bodies

In order to address the inefficiency and excessive costs of earlier organisational models used by tax administrators based mainly on "type of tax" criteria, many revenue bodies restructured their operations, adopting models based on functional principles. With the functional model, work processes and staff are organised largely within functional groupings and work across tax types. Such an approach enables greater standardisation of work processes and assists in their computerisation, thereby contributing to increased efficiency. It can also simplify dealings with taxpayers and help reduce their compliance burden. The functional approach is particularly relevant to the performance of routine tax administration tasks (e.g. taxpayer registration, accounting, inquiry services, data processing and debt collection) and organisation-wide support activities (e.g. personnel, information technology, finance and public relations). Functional organisation has been found to have a smaller impact on improving the conduct of compliance programmes, however.

Many revenue bodies around the world have begun to organise around different "taxpayer segments" and establish large taxpayer divisions. Cambodia and the Philippines, for example, have a largely functional structure, with a dedicated large taxpayer service (Figures 2.1 and 2.2).

Figure 2.1. **Organisational structure of Cambodia's General Department of Taxation**

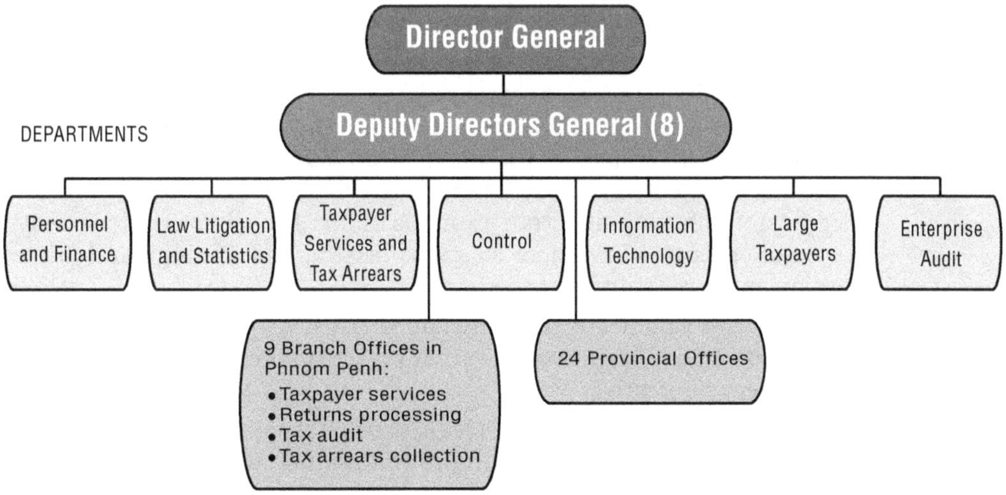

Source: General Department of Taxation (2015), "About Us", webpage, available at www.tax.gov.kh/en/aboutus.php (accessed July 2015).

Figure 2.2. **Organisational Structure of the Philippines' Bureau of Internal Revenue**

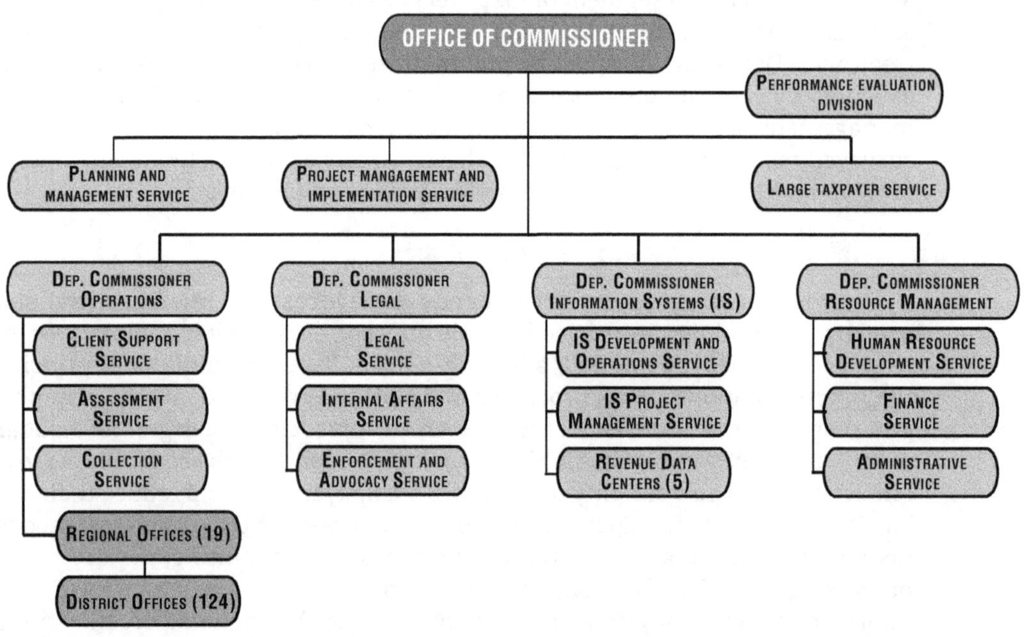

Source: Bureau of Internal Revenue (2015), "BIR Organisational Structure", website, available at www.bir.gov.ph/index.php/transparency/bir-organizational-structure.html (accessed May 2015).

Reasons for the focus on large taxpayers

The increased use of the "taxpayer segments" approach recognises the different characteristics and behaviours of each segment of taxpayers and allows for differing strategies to be taken toward each group. Among all the segments, large taxpayers are especially important due to the following reasons:

- **Large tax contribution:** Taking account of all the taxes for which they are responsible, large taxpayers typically contribute the bulk of tax revenue.
- **Complex business and tax affairs:** Large taxpayers often have complex business and tax affairs for a variety of reasons: 1) they may have multiple operating entities or operate across multiple industries; 2) they may operate in industries that raise novel or complex tax issues (e.g. oil and gas or banking); 3) their business dealings may extend across international boundaries and raise complex tax issues (e.g. profit-shifting and thin capitalisation); 4) their operations may be widely spread or located in remote locations (e.g. oil and mining); and 5) they may use complex tax planning arrangements.
- **Unique and significant tax compliance risks:** As a result of the types of factors referred to above, large taxpayers may present tax compliance risks, with significant tax revenue potential.
- **Use of professional tax experts:** Large taxpayers typically employ top-end tax experts to represent them in their tax affairs or have their own in-house tax expertise.
- **Public expectation:** Most taxpayers want to ensure that tax administrations are treating large firms appropriately.

Given these characteristics, revenue bodies in the vast majority of countries have established dedicated large taxpayer units (LTU) to manage the tax affairs of these taxpayers, with many incorporating the features set out in Box 2.1.

Box 2.1. Commonly observed features of Large Taxpayer Units (LTUs) in advanced economies

An LTU's responsibilities tend to cover both direct and indirect taxes, enabling a "whole of taxpayer" focus to be given to administering taxpayers' affairs. Business units typically provide both service and verification functions. Reflecting this and the significant revenue and compliance risks they present, considerable resources are devoted to large taxpayer administration in many economies (e.g. Australia, Canada, Italy, Japan, Mexico, the Netherlands, Poland, Spain, Turkey, the United Kingdom and the United States).

A fair number of economies have specialised industry-focused setups within their LTUs. For example:

United Kingdom: Compliance operations are organised into 17 industry-based sectors: agriculture and food, alcohol and tobacco, automotive, banking, business services, chemicals, construction, general retailing, healthcare and pharmaceuticals, insurance, leisure and media, manufacturing, oil and gas, public bodies, real estate, telecommunications and information technology, transport, and utilities.

United States: The Large Business and International (LBI) Division of the Internal Revenue Service is organised along six domestic industries and four international functions. LBI's field specialist functions are now integrated into LBI's domestic industries. The domestic industries are 1) communications, technology, and media; 2) financial services; 3) heavy manufacturing and pharmaceuticals; 4) natural resources and construction; 5) retailers, food, transportation and healthcare; and 6) global high wealth.

In addition to tax and accounting skills, specialist teams or expertise for support in areas such as industry knowledge, economics, international tax issues and computer-based examination techniques are included in the LTU. To optimise performance, considerable emphasis is given to the development of industry knowledge through the use of industry-based teams and experts for key sectors of each country's economy.

Increasing emphasis is being placed on the use of co-operative compliance strategies with large taxpayers to encourage increased levels of voluntary compliance. LTUs may use an "account manager" to provide designated large businesses with a nominated contact point for interactions with the revenue body.

Source: OECD (2015), *Tax Administration 2015: Comparative Information on OECD and Other Advanced and Emerging Economies*, http://dx.doi.org/10.1787/tax_admin-2015-en.

Major institutional reforms recently implemented or under development in the region

The **People's Republic of China**'s State Administration of Taxation reported that, since 2012, in accordance with the central government requirement to deepen reforms of administrative systems, it has been advancing organisational changes of tax bodies to accelerate their functional transformation and institutional improvement. To accommodate the demand for a "one-level tax investigation" and a specialised tax administration for large businesses, the reforms focus on: 1) optimising the assignment of working responsibilities, organisational structure and staffing; 2) streamlining superior-subordinate relationships; and 3) encouraging high-level tax bodies to assume more significant functions. The aim of the reforms is to establish a flat tax organisational system, scientifically designed functions and efficient management that adapts to reforms to the tax system and its administration, and optimises taxpayer services. Through these reforms, human resources within the tax system are expected to be more centralised, and tax administration resources are expected to be allocated in a manner that better accords with the distributional status of tax revenue sources. In addition, the reforms are expected to further improve taxpayer service and compliance.

Cambodia has already created a Large Taxpayer Division inside its General Department of Taxation. The Law on Financial Management 2016, passed in December 2015, and its regulations introduced reforms affecting the treatment of large taxpayers. First, the definition of large taxpayers has been further clarified to include enterprises with turnover exceeding KHR 2 billion (about USD 500 000), subsidiaries of foreign companies, government institutions and qualified investment project (QIP) enterprises. Second, the government fee that is required to be paid by large taxpayers to obtain a Patent Tax Certificate will now differ depending on the level of turnover. The fee for large taxpayers with turnover from KHR 2 billion to KHR 10 billion will be KHR 3 million (about USD 750), and for large taxpayers with turnover of more than KHR 10 billion will be KHR 5 million (about USD 1 250).

In **Indonesia**, the Ministry of Finance established an Oil and Gas Tax Office to oversee the administration of companies operating in the oil and gas sector in 2012. Action was also taken to unify and streamline the Foreign Enterprise and Individual Tax Office to allow it to handle all tax matters relating to foreign enterprises and individual taxpayers. In early 2015, three new senior executive positions immediately under the director general were created to strengthen executive leadership and management. The government has also decided to transform the Directorate General of Taxation into a semi-autonomous authority from the beginning of 2017, with a view to improving its effectiveness and overall administration.

Malaysia's headquarters have been restructured, and now include a Dispute Resolution Department, a Special Task Department (Investigation), and divisions for Intelligence, Risk Management, Petroleum, and Development and Facility Management. The objectives of this restructuring are to strengthen operations, simplify and expedite appeal processes, and expedite reporting and decision making. In addition, ten new Revenue Service Centres were opened in 2012 and 2013. The Inland Revenue Board of Malaysia took part in opening counters at six Urban Transformation Centres (public amenities centres established by the government for the urban community), together with other government agencies. The objectives of these changes are to provide services to the taxpayer, and to improve operational efficiency in revenue collection.

The **Maldives**' Internal Revenue Authority (MIRA) reported that numerous activities were carried out in 2013 and 2014 to improve the administration of the tax system. These included the establishment of the SAP-based ("Systems, Applications and Products") software Tax and Revenue Management System. Also, online tax returns services were set up through "MIRAconnect," which paved the way for a more convenient mechanism for taxpayers to fulfil their tax obligations. MIRAconnect was further expanded in 2015 by introducing online payment options. One of the most notable activities carried forward from 2013 was the establishment of the Large Taxpayer Service Department from January 2014. To make services more accessible, two new regional offices and collection centres were to be opened in 2015, in addition to the two existing regional offices.

In the **Philippines**, the Bureau of Internal Revenue (BIR) revealed in 2015 that the revenue body would step up monitoring of large taxpayers and address the compliance problem where relatively lower earnings were reported by a significant number of big corporations. Another problem in the Philippines related to large taxpayers is the narrow base. There are about 2 000 corporate taxpayers who account for 64% of BIR's total revenues, and the government of the Philippines intends to double the base to more than 4 000 companies.

Singapore sets up an International Tax Affairs and Relations Branch in September 2013. The branch maintains strategic oversight of the Internal Revenue Authority of Singapore's international engagement framework and programs. It drives international engagement efforts to advance Singapore's interest on the international tax front, and advises the government on international tax matters. It manages the exchange of information function, and is the liaison office for all international engagements. The International Tax Affairs and Relations Branch complements the existing Tax Policy and International Tax Division that provides technical advice in the formulation of tax policies and fair application of tax laws, reviews tax policies, initiates tax rules changes, and safeguards Singapore's economic interest through tax treaty negotiations and resolution of international tax issues.

Since 2013, **Tajikistan's** Tax Committee has been implementing a project to modernise its tax administration, supported by World Bank loan funding. The project involves reforms to organisational arrangements and business processes, and is underpinned by the use of enhanced information and communication technologies in all areas of the revenue body. A recent report prepared by the World Bank on the progress being made highlights a range of developments and matters receiving attention, including the strengthening of the audit function. The number of auditors is being increased; in the Large Taxpayer Office, the number has risen from 12 to 33.

Table 2.2 sets out details of the criteria used by revenue bodies to identify large taxpayers, the resources allocated for their administration in 2013 (expressed as full-time equivalents [FTE]), and the number of taxpayers and economic groups under administration in 2013.

Table 2.2. **Large Taxpayer Unit operations in Asian administrations**

Economy	Criteria applied to identify large taxpayers	Number of taxpayers in 2013	Dedicated staff in 2013 (FTE)	Verification results reported
Cambodia	Turnover over KHR 1 000 million	2 419	107	
China, P.R.	Cross-regional businesses, complex tax issues, or certain scale of tax revenue	45 144 (45 groups)	3 515	√
Indonesia	Weighted average of tax payment (80%) and turnover (20%) for last 3 fiscal years, and discretion by the Directorate General of Taxes	2 730	529	√
Japan	Capital over JPY 100 million	29 705	2 352	√
Kyrgyz Republic	Business income over KGS 50 million, non-business income over KGS 20 million, tax paid over KGS 2.5 million or assets over KGS 5 million	308	45	
Lao PDR	Turnover over LAK 5 billion	...	...	
Malaysia	Specific sectors	...	...	
Maldives	Top 100 business profits and GST taxpayers, along with next top 100 taxpayers and all banks	LTU set up in 2014 with 23 staff and 150 taxpayers		
Mongolia	Turnover and specific industries	398	84	√
Papua New Guinea	There is no dedicated division for managing the tax affairs of designated large taxpayers. However, the Tax Office has sections within Audit, Assessing and Advising that have large business units for managing the largest 200 taxpayers.			√
Philippines	All public corporations and others based on size (i.e. authorised capital, tax paid, annual sales, purchases and/or net worth)	2 028	610	√
Singapore	1) CIT: net tax assessed, turnover, complexity; 2) GST: annual GST supplies over SGD 100 million	CIT-1 600 GST-1 741	CIT-53 GST-25	
Tajikistan	Legal entities with annual turnover over TJS 15 million	303	77	√
Thailand	Turnover over THB 2 billion	3 450	547	

... = data not available, CIT = corporate income tax, FTE = full-time equivalents, GST = goods and services tax, Lao PDR = Lao People's Democratic Republic

Sources: ADB (2015) survey responses and OECD (2015), *Tax Administration 2015: Comparative Information on OECD and Other Advanced and Emerging Economies*, http://dx.doi.org/10.1787/tax_admin-2015-en.

Key observations

Surveys and research by the Asian Development Bank (ADB) in 2014 and 2015 as well as those presented in OECD Tax Administration 2015 (OECD, 2015) have made several key findings and observations regarding the development of large taxpayer services in Asian economies (ADB, 2016):

- The vast majority of economies covered by the surveys have established LTUs, although the data provided on resources indicates that many of these are relatively small scale and suggests that they are at an early stage of their development.
- The vast majority of revenue bodies reported having a dedicated organisational division or unit that manages the tax affairs of designated large taxpayers. Exceptions to this included Brunei Darussalam; Hong Kong, China; the Republic of Korea; Myanmar; and Papua New Guinea.
- For revenue bodies in some jurisdictions (e.g. Tajikistan), the operation of a large taxpayer office is a relatively new venture that has yet to be fully established. As a result, the level of resources allocated for administration of designated large taxpayers is relatively small (i.e. less than 1% of overall staff resources). On the other hand, there was a fair number of revenue bodies (e.g. Indonesia, Japan, the Philippines and Thailand) reporting relatively large LTU operations (i.e. more than 5% of total resources).
- Revenue bodies tend to use a mix of criteria (e.g. turnover, tax payments and specific industries) to identify taxpayers for their large taxpayer segment, although for ease of identification, a few revenue bodies (e.g. Cambodia and Japan) use a single criterion to readily identify those to be included.
- A number of revenue bodies failed to report the results of verification activities for their LTUs. This raises questions as to the scope and nature of the arrangements in place for monitoring these taxpayers' affairs.

References

ADB (2016), *A Comparative Analysis of Tax Administration in Asia and the Pacific: 2016 Edition*, Asian Development Bank, Manila.

ADB (2015), *ADB Tax Administration Survey*, Asian Development Bank, Manila.

Bureau of Internal Revenue (2015), "BIR Organisational Structure", webpage, Department of Finance, Republic of the Philippines, Manila, available at www.bir.gov.ph/index.php/transparency/bir-organizational-structure.html (accessed May 2015).

General Department of Taxation (2015), "About Us", webpage, Ministry of Economy and Finance, Royal Government of Cambodia, Phnom Penh, available at www.tax.gov.kh/en/aboutus.php (accessed July 2015).

OECD (2015), *Tax Administration 2015: Comparative Information on OECD and Other Advanced and Emerging Economies*, OECD Publishing, Paris, http://dx.doi.org/10.1787/tax_admin-2015-en.

CHAPTER 3

TAX LEVELS AND TAX STRUCTURES, 1990-2014

3.1. Comparative tables, 1990-2014

In all of the following tables (..) indicates not available. The main series in this volume cover the years 1990 to 2014.

Figures referring to 1991-95 in Table 3.1 and figures relating to 1990-96, 1998-99 and 2001-06 in Tables 3.4 to 3.19 have been omitted because of lack of space. Complete series are available on line at http://stats.oecd.org/.

Table 3.1. Total tax revenue as percentage of GDP, 1990-2014

	1990	1996	1997	1998	1999	2000	2001	2002	2003	2004
Indonesia[1]	..	..	9.1	7.4	9.3	8.6	11.9	12.3	12.9	13.2
Malaysia	19.1	19.8	20.2	17.2	16.3	14.6	18.9	18.9	17.0	16.6
Philippines	..	16.7	16.7	15.5	15.8	15.8	15.6	15.0	15.0	14.6
Singapore	..	..	..	..	..	15.5	15.1	13.1	12.7	12.3
OECD Average[2]	32.0	33.6	33.6	33.7	33.9	34.0	33.5	33.2	33.2	33.1
Japan	28.5	26.4	26.8	26.4	25.9	26.6	26.8	25.8	25.3	26.1
Korea	18.8	19.7	19.4	19.4	19.7	21.5	21.8	21.9	22.7	22.0
	2005	2006	2007	2008	2009	2010	2011	2012	2013	2014
Indonesia[1]	13.5	13.0	13.3	14.2	11.9	11.4	12.2	12.5	12.5	12.2
Malaysia	16.1	15.7	15.4	15.7	16.1	14.4	15.8	16.6	16.3	15.9
Philippines	15.2	16.5	16.3	16.2	15.0	14.8	15.1	15.8	16.2	16.7
Singapore	12.1	12.3	13.5	13.9	13.1	13.0	13.3	13.9	13.6	13.9
OECD Average[2]	33.6	33.7	33.8	33.2	32.4	32.6	33.0	33.4	33.8	34.2
Japan	27.3	28.1	28.5	28.5	27.0	27.6	28.6	29.4	30.3	32.0
Korea	22.5	23.6	24.8	24.6	23.8	23.4	24.2	24.8	24.3	24.6

.. Not available

1. The figures exclude social security contributions. The figures for social security contributions (heading 2000) are not available but they are thought to be negligible as they relate only to the "Asuransi Kesehatan" - a health insurance programme for employees in for-profit state-owned enterprises.
2. Represents the unweighted average for OECD member countries. Japan and Korea are also part of the OECD (35) group.

StatLink http://dx.doi.org/10.1787/888933428037

Table 3.2. Tax revenue of main headings as percentage of GDP, 2014

	1000 Income & profits	2000 Social security	3000 Payroll	4000 Property	5000 Goods & services	6000 Other
Indonesia[1]	5.2	..	0.0	0.2	5.4	1.4
Malaysia	10.9	0.2	0.0	0.5	3.6	0.6
Philippines	6.6	2.2	0.0	0.5	6.7	0.6
Singapore[2]	6.2	0.0	0.0	1.8	4.4	1.6
OECD Average[3]	11.5	9.1	0.4	1.9	11.0	0.2
Japan	10.2	12.7	0.0	2.7	6.3	0.1
Korea	7.2	6.6	0.1	2.7	7.4	0.7

.. Not available

1. The figures for social security contributions (heading 2000) are not available but they are thought to be negligible as they relate only to the "Asuransi Kesehatan" - a health insurance programme for employees in for-profit state-owned enterprises.
2. There are no social security contributions in Singapore.
3. Represents the unweighted average for OECD member countries. Japan and Korea are also part of the OECD (35) group.

StatLink http://dx.doi.org/10.1787/888933428042

Table 3.3. Tax revenue of main headings as percentage of total taxation, 2014

	1000 Income & profits	2000 Social security	3000 Payroll	4000 Property	5000 Goods & services	6000 Other
Indonesia[1]	42.5	..	0.0	1.8	44.4	11.3
Malaysia	68.6	1.5	0.0	3.4	22.8	3.7
Philippines	39.8	13.5	0.0	2.8	40.0	3.9
Singapore[2]	44.2	0.0	0.0	13.2	31.3	11.3
OECD Average[3]	33.7	26.2	1.1	5.6	32.6	0.7
Japan	31.8	39.7	0.0	8.5	19.8	0.3
Korea	29.1	26.9	0.3	11.0	30.0	2.8

.. Not available

1. The figures for social security contributions (heading 2000) are not available but they are thought to be negligible as they relate only to the "Asuransi Kesehatan" - a health insurance programme for employees in for-profit state-owned enterprises.
2. There are no social security contributions in Singapore.
3. Represents the unweighted average for OECD member countries. Japan and Korea are also part of the OECD (35) group.

StatLink http://dx.doi.org/10.1787/888933428056

Table 3.4. Taxes on income and profits (1000) as percentage of GDP

	1997	2000	2007	2008	2009	2010	2011	2012	2013	2014
Indonesia	4.3	4.1	6.0	6.6	5.7	5.2	5.5	5.4	5.3	5.2
Malaysia	9.8	7.7	9.9	10.3	10.6	9.1	10.8	11.5	11.2	10.9
Philippines	6.1	6.1	6.6	6.6	5.8	5.8	6.3	6.5	6.7	6.6
Singapore	..	8.2	6.1	7.1	6.2	5.8	5.9	6.2	5.9	6.2
OECD Average[1]	11.6	12.0	12.2	11.8	10.9	10.8	11.0	11.2	11.4	11.5
Japan	9.9	9.3	10.4	9.6	8.0	8.3	8.6	9.1	9.9	10.2
Korea	5.1	6.2	7.9	7.6	6.8	6.6	7.3	7.4	7.1	7.2

.. Not available

1. Represents the unweighted average for OECD member countries. Japan and Korea are also part of the OECD (35) group.

StatLink http://dx.doi.org/10.1787/888933428063

Table 3.5. Taxes on income and profits (1000) as percentage of total taxation

	1997	2000	2007	2008	2009	2010	2011	2012	2013	2014
Indonesia	47.2	47.7	45.3	46.6	47.8	45.8	45.2	43.2	42.5	42.5
Malaysia	48.6	52.7	64.0	65.4	65.6	63.4	67.9	69.1	68.6	68.6
Philippines	36.6	38.6	40.4	40.8	38.8	39.2	41.7	41.4	41.1	39.8
Singapore	..	52.8	45.4	51.1	47.0	44.7	44.7	44.7	43.1	44.2
OECD Average[1]	34.2	34.9	36.0	35.7	33.5	33.2	33.5	33.7	33.8	33.7
Japan	37.0	34.8	36.4	33.6	29.5	30.2	30.2	31.1	32.5	31.8
Korea	26.2	28.8	31.8	31.0	28.5	28.0	30.1	29.9	29.3	29.1

.. Not available

1. Represents the unweighted average for OECD member countries. Japan and Korea are also part of the OECD (35) group.

StatLink http://dx.doi.org/10.1787/888933428078

Table 3.6. Social security contributions (2000) as percentage of GDP

	1997	2000	2007	2008	2009	2010	2011	2012	2013	2014
Indonesia[1]	..	..	..	..	..	..	..	..	..	..
Malaysia	0.0	0.3	0.3	0.2	0.3	0.2	0.2	0.2	0.2	0.2
Philippines	1.4	2.1	1.9	1.8	1.9	1.9	1.9	2.0	2.1	2.2
Singapore[2]	..	0.0	0.0	0.0	0.0	0.0	0.0	0.0	0.0	0.0
OECD Average[3]	8.7	8.6	8.5	8.6	8.9	8.8	8.9	9.0	9.1	9.1
Japan	9.2	9.4	10.4	11.1	11.0	11.3	11.9	12.2	12.4	12.7
Korea	2.7	3.6	5.1	5.4	5.6	5.5	5.8	6.1	6.4	6.6

.. Not available

1. The figures for social security contributions (heading 2000) are not available but they are thought to be negligible as they relate only to the "Asuransi Kesehatan" - a health insurance programme for employees in for-profit state-owned enterprises.
2. There are no social security contributions in Singapore.
3. Represents the unweighted average for OECD member countries. Japan and Korea are also part of the OECD (35) group.

StatLink http://dx.doi.org/10.1787/888933428082

Table 3.7. Social security contributions (2000) as percentage of total taxation

	1997	2000	2007	2008	2009	2010	2011	2012	2013	2014
Indonesia[1]	..	..	..	..	..	..	..	..	..	..
Malaysia	0.0	1.9	1.6	1.5	1.6	1.7	1.5	1.4	1.5	1.5
Philippines	8.1	13.1	11.8	11.3	12.9	12.7	12.7	12.9	12.7	13.5
Singapore[2]	..	0.0	0.0	0.0	0.0	0.0	0.0	0.0	0.0	0.0
OECD Average[3]	25.1	24.8	24.7	25.5	26.8	26.6	26.4	26.4	26.3	26.2
Japan	34.2	35.2	36.5	38.8	41.0	41.1	41.5	41.6	40.8	39.7
Korea	14.2	16.7	20.7	21.8	23.4	23.3	24.0	24.7	26.4	26.9

.. Not available

1. The figures for social security contributions (heading 2000) are not available but they are thought to be negligible as they relate only to the "Asuransi Kesehatan" - a health insurance programme for employees in for-profit state-owned enterprises.
2. There are no social security contributions in Singapore.
3. Represents the unweighted average for OECD member countries. Japan and Korea are also part of the OECD (35) group.

StatLink http://dx.doi.org/10.1787/888933428090

Table 3.8. Taxes on property (4000) as percentage of GDP

	1997	2000	2007	2008	2009	2010	2011	2012	2013	2014
Indonesia	0.4	0.3	0.8	0.6	0.5	0.5	0.4	0.3	0.3	0.2
Malaysia	0.5	0.5	0.6	0.6	0.6	0.6	0.5	0.5	0.5	0.5
Philippines	0.2	0.5	0.5	0.4	0.5	0.4	0.5	0.5	0.5	0.5
Singapore	..	1.7	2.3	1.6	1.6	1.9	2.0	2.2	2.2	1.8
OECD Average[1]	1.7	1.8	1.8	1.7	1.7	1.7	1.8	1.8	1.9	1.9
Japan	3.0	2.8	2.6	2.7	2.7	2.7	2.8	2.7	2.7	2.7
Korea	2.5	2.7	3.2	2.9	2.8	2.6	2.7	2.6	2.5	2.7

.. Not available

1. Represents the unweighted average for OECD member countries. Japan and Korea are also part of the OECD (35) group.

StatLink http://dx.doi.org/10.1787/888933428104

Table 3.9. Taxes on property (4000) as percentage of total taxation

	1997	2000	2007	2008	2009	2010	2011	2012	2013	2014
Indonesia	4.2	3.7	5.6	4.4	4.6	4.7	3.1	2.7	2.1	1.8
Malaysia	2.5	3.4	4.0	3.6	3.9	4.0	3.5	3.2	3.2	3.4
Philippines	0.9	3.1	2.9	2.7	3.1	2.9	3.0	3.1	3.0	2.8
Singapore	..	11.2	17.1	11.5	11.9	14.5	15.4	16.1	15.9	13.2
OECD Average[1]	5.3	5.5	5.6	5.3	5.5	5.5	5.5	5.5	5.6	5.6
Japan	11.2	10.5	9.0	9.4	10.1	9.7	9.7	9.1	8.8	8.5
Korea	12.7	12.4	12.8	11.9	11.6	11.3	11.4	10.6	10.3	11.0

.. Not available

1. Represents the unweighted average for OECD member countries. Japan and Korea are also part of the OECD (35) group.

StatLink http://dx.doi.org/10.1787/888933428118

Table 3.10. Taxes on goods and services (5000) as percentage of GDP

	1997	2000	2007	2008	2009	2010	2011	2012	2013	2014
Indonesia	4.3	3.9	5.6	6.0	4.8	4.7	5.2	5.6	5.7	5.4
Malaysia	8.9	5.6	4.1	4.2	4.2	3.9	3.7	3.8	3.7	3.6
Philippines	8.4	6.6	6.6	6.6	6.2	6.1	5.9	6.1	6.4	6.7
Singapore	..	4.8	4.4	4.5	4.5	4.5	4.4	4.2	4.2	4.4
OECD Average[1]	10.9	10.9	10.6	10.3	10.3	10.6	10.6	10.8	10.8	11.0
Japan	4.6	5.1	5.1	5.1	5.1	5.1	5.3	5.3	5.3	6.3
Korea	8.3	8.2	7.8	7.8	7.6	7.9	7.5	7.7	7.5	7.4

.. Not available

1. Represents the unweighted average for OECD member countries. Japan and Korea are also part of the OECD (35) group.

StatLink http://dx.doi.org/10.1787/888933428127

Table 3.11. Taxes on goods and services (5000) as percentage of total taxation

	1997	2000	2007	2008	2009	2010	2011	2012	2013	2014
Indonesia	47.6	44.7	41.9	42.3	40.4	41.8	42.9	44.8	45.4	44.4
Malaysia	44.0	38.4	26.8	26.6	25.9	27.3	23.6	22.7	22.8	22.8
Philippines	50.2	42.0	40.7	40.7	41.4	41.3	38.7	38.8	39.4	40.0
Singapore	..	31.1	32.9	32.2	34.5	34.4	32.8	30.5	30.8	31.3
OECD Average[1]	33.4	33.0	31.9	31.6	32.3	32.9	32.7	32.6	32.4	32.6
Japan	17.2	19.3	18.0	17.9	19.1	18.7	18.4	18.0	17.6	19.8
Korea	42.7	38.4	31.3	31.6	31.8	33.7	31.2	31.2	30.7	30.0

.. Not available

1. Represents the unweighted average for OECD member countries. Japan and Korea are also part of the OECD (35) group.

StatLink http://dx.doi.org/10.1787/888933428133

Table 3.12. Taxes on general consumption (5110) as percentage of GDP

	1997	2000	2007	2008	2009	2010	2011	2012	2013	2014
Indonesia	3.2	2.5	3.9	4.2	3.4	3.4	3.5	3.9	4.0	3.9
Malaysia	2.2	1.7	1.0	1.1	1.2	1.0	0.9	1.0	1.0	1.0
Philippines	1.8	1.5	2.1	1.8	2.1	1.9	1.9	2.2	2.2	2.2
Singapore	..	1.3	2.3	2.4	2.5	2.5	2.5	2.5	2.5	2.6
OECD Average[1]	6.6	6.7	6.8	6.6	6.4	6.7	6.7	6.8	6.8	7.0
Japan	1.9	2.4	2.5	2.5	2.6	2.6	2.7	2.7	2.8	3.9
Korea	3.7	3.7	3.9	4.0	4.1	4.1	4.1	4.3	4.1	4.2

.. Not available

1. Represents the unweighted average for OECD member countries. Japan and Korea are also part of the OECD (35) group.

StatLink http://dx.doi.org/10.1787/888933428148

Table 3.13. Taxes on general consumption (5110) as percentage of total taxation

	1997	2000	2007	2008	2009	2010	2011	2012	2013	2014
Indonesia	35.5	29.4	29.4	29.8	29.0	29.6	29.1	31.4	32.3	31.8
Malaysia	10.8	11.5	6.5	6.9	7.5	6.9	5.9	5.9	6.1	6.2
Philippines	10.6	9.5	12.9	11.2	14.0	13.0	12.5	13.8	13.4	13.2
Singapore	..	8.3	16.8	17.2	18.9	19.6	18.9	18.0	18.6	18.9
OECD Average[1]	20.1	19.9	20.2	20.1	20.1	20.7	20.6	20.5	20.5	20.7
Japan	7.2	9.1	8.8	8.9	9.6	9.6	9.4	9.2	9.2	12.2
Korea	18.9	17.0	15.8	16.1	17.2	17.5	17.0	17.2	17.0	17.2

.. Not available

1. Represents the unweighted average for OECD member countries. Japan and Korea are also part of the OECD (35) group.

StatLink http://dx.doi.org/10.1787/888933428156

Table 3.14. Taxes on specific goods and services (5120) as percentage of GDP

	1997	2000	2007	2008	2009	2010	2011	2012	2013	2014
Indonesia	1.1	1.3	1.7	1.8	1.3	1.4	1.7	1.7	1.6	1.5
Malaysia	5.4	2.9	2.5	2.5	2.4	2.4	2.3	2.3	2.2	2.2
Philippines	6.5	5.0	4.4	4.7	4.0	4.1	3.9	3.9	4.1	4.4
Singapore	..	2.0	1.4	1.4	1.4	1.3	1.3	1.2	1.2	1.3
OECD Average[1]	3.7	3.6	3.2	3.1	3.2	3.3	3.3	3.3	3.3	3.3
Japan	2.1	2.1	2.0	2.0	2.0	2.0	2.0	2.0	2.0	1.9
Korea	4.2	4.2	3.6	3.6	3.2	3.5	2.9	3.0	2.9	2.7

.. Not available

1. Represents the unweighted average for OECD member countries. Japan and Korea are also part of the OECD (35) group.

StatLink http://dx.doi.org/10.1787/888933428160

Table 3.15. Taxes on specific goods and services (5120) as percentage of total taxation

	1997	2000	2007	2008	2009	2010	2011	2012	2013	2014
Indonesia	12.1	15.3	12.5	12.5	11.3	12.2	13.8	13.5	13.1	12.6
Malaysia	26.8	19.8	16.5	16.2	14.7	16.6	14.4	13.7	13.7	13.6
Philippines	39.1	32.0	27.0	28.8	26.7	27.0	25.6	24.5	25.4	26.2
Singapore	..	13.0	10.1	10.2	10.5	10.3	9.8	8.9	8.9	9.5
OECD Average[1]	11.5	11.1	9.7	9.6	10.1	10.2	10.0	10.0	9.8	9.6
Japan	7.9	8.0	7.1	6.9	7.3	7.2	7.1	6.9	6.7	6.0
Korea	21.6	19.7	14.5	14.5	13.6	15.1	12.2	12.0	11.8	10.8

.. Not available

1. Represents the unweighted average for OECD member countries. Japan and Korea are also part of the OECD (35) group.

StatLink http://dx.doi.org/10.1787/888933428179

Table 3.16. Gross domestic product for tax reporting years at market prices, in billions of national currency units

	1997	2000	2007	2008	2009	2010	2011	2012	2013	2014
Indonesia	627 696	1 389 770	3 950 893	4 948 688	5 606 203	6 864 133	7 831 726	8 615 705	9 546 134	10 565 817
Malaysia	282	356	665	770	713	821	912	971	1 019	1 107
Philippines	2 689	3 581	6 893	7 721	8 026	9 004	9 708	10 561	11 538	12 645
Singapore	149	165	271	272	280	322	346	362	376	388
OECD member countries										
Japan	521 295	510 835	513 023	489 520	473 996	480 528	474 171	474 404	482 401	489 558
Korea	530 347	635 185	1 043 258	1 104 492	1 151 708	1 265 308	1 332 681	1 377 457	1 429 445	1 486 079

Source: National statistical offices, and CEIC for Indonesia, Malaysia, the Philippines and Singapore and OECD National Accounts data for Japan and Korea.

StatLink http://dx.doi.org/10.1787/888933428180

Table 3.17. Gross domestic product for tax reporting years at market prices, in millions of US Dollars at market exchange rates

	1997	2000	2007	2008	2009	2010	2011	2012	2013	2014
Indonesia	217 906	165 612	432 295	510 582	538 639	755 392	892 401	918 104	912 590	890 227
Malaysia	99 957	93 790	193 694	231 158	202 372	255 302	298 277	314 661	323 370	338 110
Philippines	91 236	81 019	149 363	173 601	168 484	199 597	224 142	250 085	271 844	284 825
Singapore	100 038	95 732	180 033	192 099	192 453	236 451	274 922	289 585	300 201	306 449
OECD member countries										
Japan	4 308 348	4 737 202	4 356 697	4 734 782	5 065 603	5 475 432	5 948 938	5 943 896	4 942 730	4 625 123
Korea	557 962	561 792	1 122 446	1 003 298	903 338	1 095 096	1 203 539	1 223 389	1 305 518	1 411 196

Note: This table is produced based on GDP data in national currency from Table 3.16 and exchange rate data from Table 3.19.

StatLink http://dx.doi.org/10.1787/888933428194

Table 3.18. Total tax revenue in millions of US Dollars at market exchange rates

	1997	2000	2007	2008	2009	2010	2011	2012	2013	2014
Indonesia	19 906	14 264	57 550	72 573	63 897	85 782	108 615	114 616	113 930	108 323
Malaysia	20 185	13 647	29 889	36 300	32 578	36 768	47 207	52 334	52 784	53 614
Philippines	15 201	12 769	24 305	28 200	25 303	29 502	33 928	39 529	44 024	47 561
Singapore	..	14 849	24 312	26 634	25 180	30 696	36 592	40 148	40 862	42 718
OECD member countries										
Japan	1 152 932	1 262 348	1 241 928	1 350 408	1 365 456	1 509 557	1 702 089	1 748 801	1 500 043	1 482 010
Korea	108 274	120 547	278 198	247 262	214 634	256 154	290 720	303 158	317 220	347 014

.. Not available

Note: This table is produced based on total tax revenues from Chapter 4 and exchange rate data from Table 3.19.

StatLink http://dx.doi.org/10.1787/888933428205

Table 3.19. Exchange rates used, national currency per US dollar

	1997	2000	2007	2008	2009	2010	2011	2012	2013	2014
Indonesia	2 880.60	8 391.70	9 139.40	9 692.30	10 408.10	9 086.90	8 776.00	9 384.20	10 460.50	11 868.70
Malaysia	2.80	3.80	3.40	3.30	3.50	3.20	3.10	3.10	3.20	3.30
Philippines	29.50	44.20	46.10	44.50	47.60	45.10	43.30	42.20	42.40	44.40
Singapore	1.50	1.70	1.50	1.40	1.50	1.40	1.30	1.20	1.30	1.30
OECD member countries										
Japan	121.00	107.80	117.80	103.40	93.60	87.80	79.70	79.80	97.60	105.80
Korea	950.50	1 130.60	929.50	1 100.90	1 274.90	1 155.40	1 107.30	1 125.90	1 094.90	1 053.10

Source: National statistical offices, and CEIC for Indonesia, Malaysia, the Philippines and Singapore and OECD National Accounts data for Japan and Korea.

StatLink http://dx.doi.org/10.1787/888933428218

3.2. Comparative figures

Figure 3.1. **Tax revenue of main headings as % of total tax revenue, 2014**

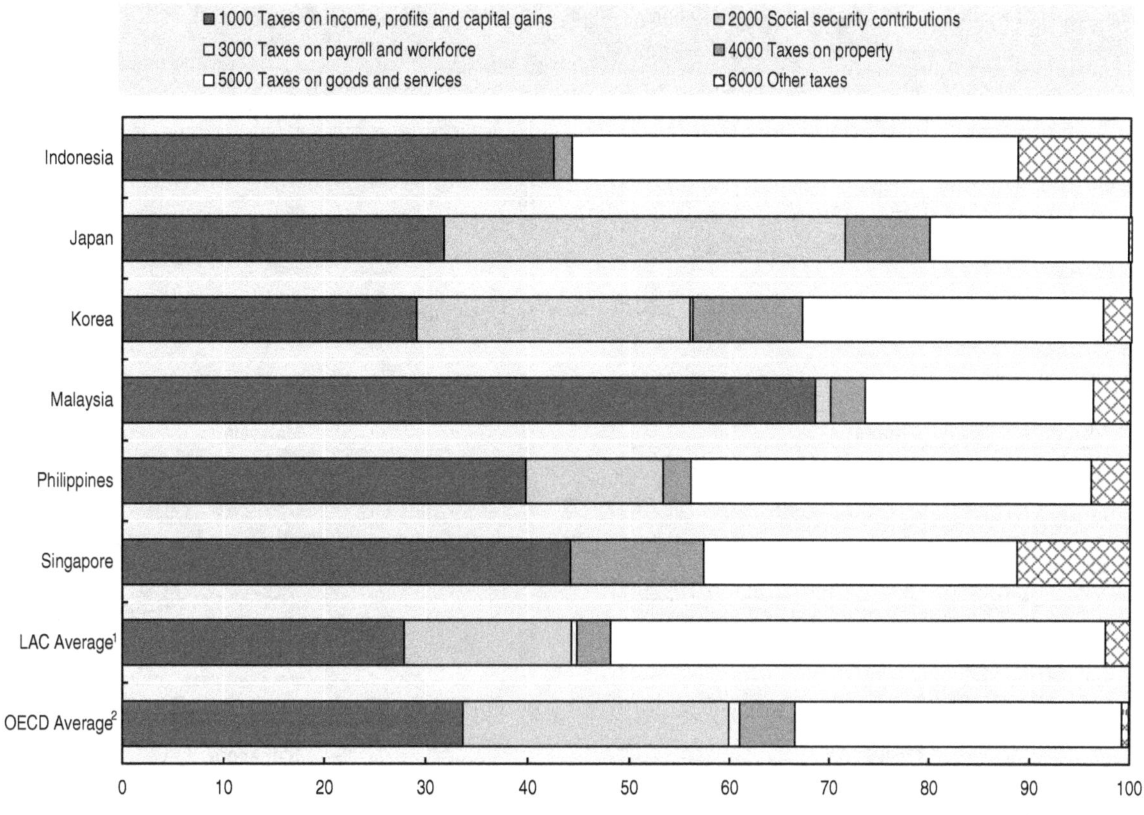

1. Represents the unweighted average for 22 LAC (Latin American and Caribbean) countries.

2. Represents the unweighted average for OECD member countries. Japan and Korea are also part of the OECD (35) group.

Source: Table 3.3.

StatLink http://dx.doi.org/10.1787/888933428003

Figure 3.2. **Tax structures, 1990-2014**

Receipts as percentage of total tax revenues

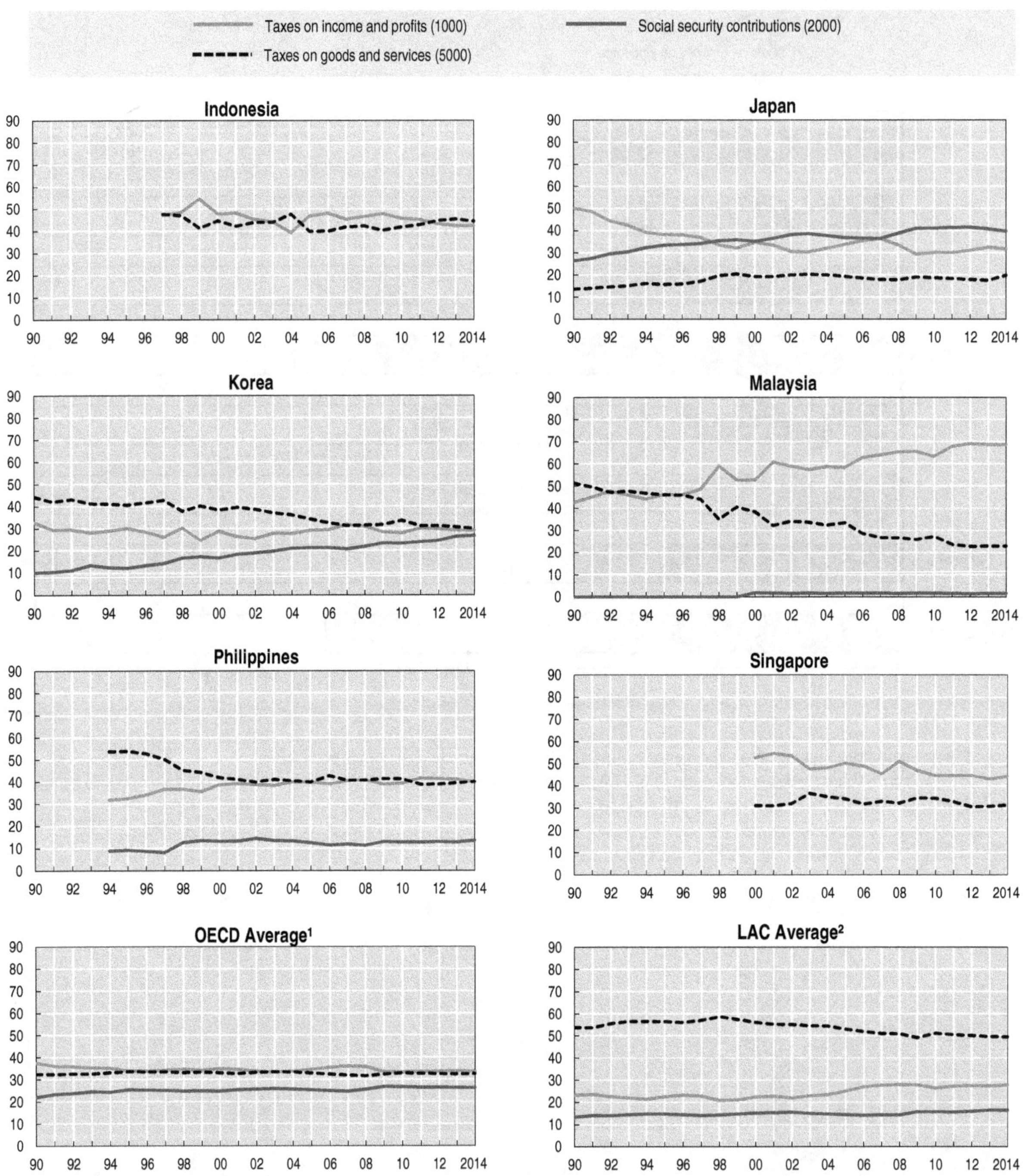

1. Represents the unweighted average for OECD member countries. Japan and Korea are also part of the OECD (35) group.
2. Represents the unweighted average for 22 LAC (Latin American and Caribbean) countries.
Source: Tables in Chapter 3.

StatLink http://dx.doi.org/10.1787/888933428013

CHAPTER 4

COUNTRY TABLES, 1997-2014 – TAX REVENUES

Table 4.1. Indonesia
Details of tax revenue

Billion IDR

	1997	2000	2007	2008	2009	2010	2011	2012	2013	2014
Total tax revenue	**57 340**	**119 697**	**525 969**	**703 394**	**665 047**	**779 484**	**953 206**	**1 075 584**	**1 191 766**	**1 285 655**
1000 Taxes on income, profits and capital gains	**27 062**	**57 073**	**238 431**	**327 498**	**317 615**	**357 046**	**431 122**	**465 070**	**506 443**	**546 181**
1100 Of individuals	..	..	77 250	96 002	107 632	122 031	150 537	171 210	197 987	238 058
1110 On income and profits	..	..	..	..	..	..	..	..	..	..
1120 On capital gains	..	..	..	..	..	..	..	..	..	..
1200 Corporate	..	..	161 181	231 496	209 983	235 015	280 585	293 859	308 456	308 123
1210 On profits	..	..	..	..	..	..	..	..	..	..
1220 On capital gains	..	..	..	..	..	..	..	..	..	..
1300 Unallocable between 1100 and 1200	27 062	57 073	0	0	0	0	0	0	0	0
2000 Social security contributions	..	..	..	..	..	..	..	..	..	..
2100 Employees	..	..	..	..	..	..	..	..	..	..
2110 On a payroll basis	..	..	..	..	..	..	..	..	..	..
2120 On an income tax basis	..	..	..	..	..	..	..	..	..	..
2200 Employers	..	..	..	..	..	..	..	..	..	..
2210 On a payroll basis	..	..	..	..	..	..	..	..	..	..
2220 On an income tax basis	..	..	..	..	..	..	..	..	..	..
2300 Self-employed or non-employed	..	..	..	..	..	..	..	..	..	..
2310 On a payroll basis	..	..	..	..	..	..	..	..	..	..
2320 On an income tax basis	..	..	..	..	..	..	..	..	..	..
2400 Unallocable between 2100, 2200 and 2300	..	..	..	..	..	..	..	..	..	..
2410 On a payroll basis	..	..	..	..	..	..	..	..	..	..
2420 On an income tax basis	..	..	..	..	..	..	..	..	..	..
3000 Taxes on payroll and workforce	**0**	**0**	**0**	**0**	**0**	**0**	**0**	**0**	**0**	**0**
4000 Taxes on property	**2 413**	**4 456**	**29 677**	**30 927**	**30 735**	**36 607**	**29 892**	**28 969**	**25 305**	**23 476**
4100 Recurrent taxes on immovable property	2 413	3 525	23 724	25 354	24 270	28 581	29 893	28 969	25 305	23 476
4110 Households	..	..	..	..	..	..	..	..	..	..
4120 Others	..	..	..	..	..	..	..	..	..	..
4200 Recurrent taxes on net wealth	0	0	0	0	0	0	0	0	0	0
4210 Individual	..	..	..	..	..	..	..	..	..	..
4220 Corporate	..	..	..	..	..	..	..	..	..	..
4300 Estate, inheritance and gift taxes	0	0	0	0	0	0	0	0	0	0
4310 Estate and inheritance taxes	..	..	..	..	..	..	..	..	..	..
4320 Gift taxes	..	..	..	..	..	..	..	..	..	..
4400 Taxes on financial and capital transactions	0	931	5 953	5 573	6 465	8 026	-1	0	0	0
Tax on acquisition of land and buildings	..	931	5 953	5 573	6 465	8 026	-1	..	..	..
4500 Non-recurrent taxes	0	0	0	0	0	0	0	0	0	0
4510 On net wealth	..	..	..	..	..	..	..	..	..	..
4520 Other non-recurrent taxes	..	..	..	..	..	..	..	..	..	..
4600 Other recurrent taxes on property	0	0	0	0	0	0	0	0	0	0
5000 Taxes on goods and services	**27 274**	**53 547**	**220 143**	**297 241**	**268 456**	**325 685**	**408 932**	**482 269**	**540 622**	**570 915**
5100 Taxes on production, sale, transfer, etc	27 274	53 547	220 143	297 241	268 456	325 685	408 932	482 269	540 622	570 915
5110 General taxes	20 351	35 232	154 527	209 647	193 068	230 605	277 800	337 585	384 714	409 182
5111 Value added taxes	20 351	35 232	154 527	209 647	193 068	230 605	277 800	337 585	384 714	409 182
5112 Sales tax	0	0	0	0	0	0	0	0	0	0
5113 Other	0	0	0	0	0	0	0	0	0	0
5120 Taxes on specific goods and services	6 923	18 315	65 616	87 594	75 389	95 080	131 131	144 684	155 909	161 734
5121 Excises	4 263	11 287	44 679	51 252	56 718	66 166	77 010	95 028	108 452	118 086
5122 Profits of fiscal monopolies	0	0	0	0	0	0	0	0	0	0
5123 Customs and import duties	2 579	6 697	16 699	22 764	18 105	20 017	25 266	28 418	31 621	32 319
5124 Taxes on exports	81	331	4 237	13 578	565	8 898	28 856	21 238	15 835	11 329
5125 Taxes on investment goods	0	0	0	0	0	0	0	0	0	0
5126 Taxes on specific services	0	0	0	0	0	0	0	0	0	0
5127 Other taxes on internat. trade and transactions	0	0	0	0	0	0	0	0	0	0
5128 Other taxes	0	0	0	0	0	0	0	0	0	0
5130 Unallocable between 5110 and 5120	0	0	0	0	0	0	0	0	0	0
5200 Taxes on use of goods and to perform activities	0	0	0	0	0	0	0	0	0	0
5210 Recurrent taxes	..	..	..	..	..	..	..	..	..	..
5211 Paid by households: motor vehicles	..	..	..	..	..	..	..	..	..	..
5212 Paid by others: motor vehicles	..	..	..	..	..	..	..	..	..	..
5213 Paid in respect of other goods	..	..	..	..	..	..	..	..	..	..
5220 Non-recurrent taxes	..	..	..	..	..	..	..	..	..	..
5300 Unallocable between 5100 and 5200	0	0	0	0	0	0	0	0	0	0
6000 Other taxes	**591**	**4 621**	**37 718**	**47 728**	**48 241**	**60 146**	**83 260**	**99 276**	**119 397**	**145 082**
6100 Paid solely by business	0	0	0	0	0	0	0	0	0	0
6200 Other	591	4 621	37 718	47 728	48 241	60 146	83 260	99 276	119 397	145 082
Other local level	0	3 784	34 981	44 693	45 125	56 177	79 332	95 066	114 460	138 789
Other non local level	591	837	2 738	3 034	3 116	3 969	3 928	4 211	4 937	6 293

Note:

Year ending 31st December.

The data are on a cash basis.

The figures for social security contributions (heading 2000) are not available but they are thought to be negligible as they relate only to the "Asuransi Kesehatan" - a health insurance programme for employees in for-profit state-owned enterprises.

Source: Ministry of Finance of the Republic of Indonesia.

StatLink http://dx.doi.org/10.1787/888933428227

Table 4.2. Japan
Details of tax revenue

Billion JPY

	1997	2000	2007	2008	2009	2010	2011	2012	2013	2014
Total tax revenue	**139 501**	**136 125**	**146 243**	**139 616**	**127 768**	**132 480**	**135 668**	**139 578**	**146 401**	**156 867**
1000 Taxes on income, profits and capital gains	**51 673**	**47 398**	**53 174**	**46 850**	**37 739**	**40 034**	**40 910**	**43 352**	**47 534**	**49 939**
1100 Of individuals	29 809	28 677	28 600	27 790	25 518	24 663	24 951	25 946	28 150	29 655
1110 On income and profits	29 809	28 677	28 600	27 790	25 518	24 663	24 951	25 946	28 150	29 655
Income tax	19 183	18 789	16 080	14 985	12 914	12 984	13 476	14 044	15 865	17 139
Prefectural inhabitants tax	3 183	3 621	5 008	5 143	5 052	4 699	4 608	4 783	5 090	5 215
Municipal inhabitants tax	7 172	6 044	7 294	7 445	7 349	6 795	6 688	6 942	7 015	7 114
Enterprise tax	271	223	218	217	204	184	179	178	181	186
1120 On capital gains	0	0	0	0	0	0	0	0	0	0
1200 Corporate	21 864	18 721	24 573	19 061	12 221	15 372	15 959	17 406	19 384	20 284
1210 On profits	21 864	18 721	24 573	19 061	12 221	15 372	15 959	17 406	19 384	20 284
Corporation tax	13 477	11 747	14 744	10 011	6 356	8 968	9 351	10 408	11 698	11 464
Prefectural inhabitants tax	1 026	879	1 206	1 096	715	777	800	846	854	963
Municipal inhabitants tax	2 532	2 176	3 015	2 752	1 775	1 954	2 011	2 129	2 157	2 445
Enterprise tax	4 830	3 918	5 608	5 203	2 701	2 253	2 240	2 354	2 674	3 017
Local special corporate tax	0	0	0	0	674	1 420	1 556	1 670	2 001	2 395
Local corporate tax	0	0	0	0	0	0	0	0	0	1
1220 On capital gains	0	0	0	0	0	0	0	0	0	0
1300 Unallocable between 1100 and 1200	0	0	0	0	0	0	0	0	0	0
2000 Social security contributions	**47 744**	**47 857**	**53 321**	**54 227**	**52 342**	**54 456**	**56 321**	**58 068**	**59 800**	**62 232**
2100 Employees	19 642	19 786	21 972	23 250	22 484	23 590	24 431	25 182	25 982	27 146
2110 On a payroll basis	19 642	19 786	21 972	23 250	22 484	23 590	24 431	25 182	25 982	27 146
2120 On an income tax basis	0	0	0	0	0	0	0	0	0	0
2200 Employers	22 750	22 388	24 240	24 663	23 575	24 672	25 735	26 333	27 141	28 394
2210 On a payroll basis	22 750	22 388	24 240	24 663	23 575	24 672	25 735	26 333	27 141	28 394
2220 On an income tax basis	0	0	0	0	0	0	0	0	0	0
2300 Self-employed or non-employed	5 352	5 683	7 108	6 314	6 282	6 194	6 156	6 553	6 676	6 693
2310 On a payroll basis	5 352	5 683	7 108	6 314	6 282	6 194	6 156	6 553	6 676	6 693
2320 On an income tax basis	0	0	0	0	0	0	0	0	0	0
2400 Unallocable between 2100, 2200 and 2300	0	0	0	0	0	0	0	0	0	0
2410 On a payroll basis	..	..	..	..	..	..	..	..	..	..
2420 On an income tax basis	..	..	..	..	..	..	..	..	..	..
3000 Taxes on payroll and workforce	**0**	**0**	**0**	**0**	**0**	**0**	**0**	**0**	**0**	**0**
4000 Taxes on property	**15 679**	**14 294**	**13 138**	**13 111**	**12 949**	**12 878**	**13 100**	**12 716**	**12 940**	**13 306**
4100 Recurrent taxes on immovable property	10 410	10 414	9 949	10 123	10 128	10 225	10 237	9 799	9 882	10 016
Prefectural property tax	8	11	14	18	19	5	3	2	2	2
Municipal property tax	8 822	9 041	8 729	8 876	8 874	8 961	8 966	8 580	8 653	8 769
City planning tax	1 326	1 318	1 202	1 225	1 233	1 256	1 268	1 216	1 227	1 244
Special landholding tax	94	43	4	4	2	3	1	1	1	2
Water and land utilisation tax	0	0	0	0	0	0	0	0	0	0
Land value tax	160	1	0	0	0	0	0	0	0	0
4110 Households	..	..	..	..	..	..	..	..	..	..
4120 Others	..	..	..	..	..	..	..	..	..	..
4200 Recurrent taxes on net wealth	0	0	0	0	0	0	0	0	0	0
4210 Individual	..	..	..	..	..	..	..	..	..	..
4220 Corporate	..	..	..	..	..	..	..	..	..	..
4300 Estate, inheritance and gift taxes	2 413	1 782	1 503	1 455	1 350	1 250	1 474	1 504	1 574	1 883
4310 Estate and inheritance taxes	..	..	..	..	..	..	..	..	..	..
Inheritance tax	..	..	..	..	..	..	..	..	..	..
4320 Gift taxes	..	..	..	..	..	..	..	..	..	..
Tax on gifts	..	..	..	..	..	..	..	..	..	..
4400 Taxes on financial and capital transactions	2 856	2 099	1 686	1 534	1 472	1 403	1 388	1 413	1 483	1 407
Bourse tax	40	0	0	0	0	0	0	0	0	0
Securities transaction	404	0	0	0	0	0	0	0	0	0
Bank of Japan note issue tax	0	0	0	0	0	0	0	0	0	0
Stamp revenues	1 681	1 532	1 202	1 088	1 068	1 024	1 047	1 078	1 126	1 035
Real property acquisition tax	731	567	485	445	404	379	342	336	357	372
4500 Non-recurrent taxes	0	0	0	0	0	0	0	0	0	0
4510 On net wealth	..	..	..	..	..	..	..	..	..	..
4520 Other non-recurrent taxes	..	..	..	..	..	..	..	..	..	..
4600 Other recurrent taxes on property	0	0	0	0	0	0	0	0	0	0
5000 Taxes on goods and services	**24 058**	**26 227**	**26 256**	**25 060**	**24 364**	**24 730**	**24 966**	**25 056**	**25 744**	**30 991**
5100 Taxes on production, sale, transfer, etc	21 132	23 180	23 241	22 111	21 561	22 160	22 410	22 592	23 313	28 587
5110 General taxes	10 112	12 350	12 841	12 443	12 221	12 675	12 745	12 902	13 479	19 135
5111 Value added taxes	10 112	12 350	12 841	12 443	12 221	12 675	12 745	12 902	13 479	19 135
5112 Sales tax	0	0	0	0	0	0	0	0	0	0
5113 Other	0	0	0	0	0	0	0	0	0	0
5120 Taxes on specific goods and services	11 021	10 830	10 400	9 668	9 340	9 485	9 665	9 690	9 834	9 452

Table 4.2. Japan (cont.)
Details of tax revenue

Billion JPY

	1997	2000	2007	2008	2009	2010	2011	2012	2013	2014
5121 Excises	9 764	9 837	9 374	8 702	8 527	8 622	8 719	8 721	8 728	8 308
Liquor tax	1 962	1 816	1 524	1 461	1 417	1 389	1 369	1 350	1 371	1 328
Sugar excises	0	0	0	0	0	0	0	0	0	0
Local gasoline tax	276	296	302	286	291	294	283	281	275	266
Gasoline tax	2 583	2 769	2 820	2 572	2 715	2 750	2 648	2 622	2 574	2 486
Liquefied petroleum gas tax	29	28	27	26	25	24	23	21	21	19
Aviation fuel tax	104	104	104	99	94	89	60	64	67	67
Commodity tax	0	0	0	0	0	0	0	0	0	0
Playing-card tax	0	0	0	0	0	0	0	0	0	0
Prefectural tobacco tax	248	282	278	263	250	256	293	289	173	155
Municipal tobacco tax	799	865	853	808	767	788	900	887	983	950
Timber delivery tax	0	0	0	0	0	0	0	0	0	0
Mineral product tax	2	2	2	2	2	2	2	2	2	2
Electricity and gas tax	0	0	0	0	0	0	0	0	0	0
Diesel oil tax	1 331	1 208	1 034	919	908	918	932	925	943	936
Vehicle acquisition tax	562	464	425	366	231	192	168	210	193	86
Promotion of power resources development tax	354	375	352	341	329	349	331	328	328	321
Petroleum and coal tax	497	489	513	511	487	502	519	567	600	631
Tobacco tax	1 018	876	925	851	822	908	1 032	1 018	1 038	919
Special tobacco tax	0	264	214	197	190	163	160	158	161	142
5122 Profits of fiscal monopolies	0	0	0	0	0	0	0	0	0	0
Monopoly profits	..	..	..	..	..	..	..	..	..	..
5123 Customs and import duties	1 012	877	941	883	732	786	874	897	1 034	1 073
Customs duty	1 012	877	941	883	732	786	874	897	1 034	1 073
5124 Taxes on exports	0	0	0	0	0	0	0	0	0	0
5125 Taxes on investment goods	0	0	0	0	0	0	0	0	0	0
5126 Taxes on specific services	245	116	85	84	81	77	72	73	71	70
Travel tax	0	0	0	0	0	0	0	0	0	0
Admission tax	0	0	0	0	0	0	0	0	0	0
Local entertainment tax	0	0	0	0	0	0	0	0	0	0
Golf course utilisation tax	98	81	60	60	58	55	51	51	49	48
Meal and lodging tax	0	0	0	0	0	0	0	0	0	0
Special local consumption tax	125	12	0	0	0	0	0	0	0	0
Bathing tax	22	23	25	24	23	22	21	22	22	22
5127 Other taxes on internat. trade and transactions	0	0	0	0	0	0	0	0	0	0
5128 Other taxes	0	0	0	0	0	0	0	0	0	0
5130 Unallocable between 5110 and 5120	0	0	0	0	0	0	0	0	0	0
5200 Taxes on use of goods and to perform activities	2 926	3 047	3 015	2 949	2 803	2 570	2 557	2 464	2 431	2 404
5210 Recurrent taxes	2 905	3 027	2 993	2 928	2 783	2 548	2 535	2 442	2 409	2 382
Automobile tax	1 705	1 765	1 717	1 681	1 654	1 616	1 597	1 586	1 574	1 556
Light vehicle tax	113	125	164	169	174	178	180	184	189	195
Motor vehicle tonnage tax	1 084	1 134	1 110	1 076	953	753	755	669	643	629
Hunter licence tax	2	2	0	0	0	0	0	0	0	0
Hunting tax	1	1	2	2	2	2	2	2	2	2
Mine lot tax	1	1	0	0	0	0	0	0	0	0
5211 Paid by households: motor vehicles	..	..	..	..	..	..	..	..	..	..
5212 Paid by others: motor vehicles	..	..	..	..	..	..	..	..	..	..
5213 Paid in respect of other goods	..	..	..	..	..	..	..	..	..	..
5220 Non-recurrent taxes	21	20	22	21	20	21	22	22	22	23
5300 Unallocable between 5100 and 5200	0	0	0	0	0	0	0	0	0	0
6000 Other taxes	**346**	**348**	**356**	**367**	**374**	**381**	**371**	**386**	**384**	**399**
6100 Paid solely by business	325	324	313	323	328	330	339	350	348	356
Business office tax	325	324	313	323	328	330	339	350	348	356
6200 Other	22	24	43	45	46	52	32	36	36	43
Taxes not in local tax law	21	24	43	45	46	52	32	36	36	43
Other	0	0	0	0	0	0	0	0	0	0

Note:

Data are on a fiscal year basis beginning 1st April.

From 1990, data are on an accrual basis.

The figures for different groups of taxes are reported on different reporting bases, namely: Social security contributions (heading 2000) : in principle accrual basis, Central government taxes : accrual basis (revenues accrued during the fiscal year plus cash receipts collected before the end of May (the end of April until 1977), Local government taxes : accrual basis (due to be paid during the fiscal year and cash receipts collected before the end of May).

The Japanese authorities take the view that the Enterprise tax (classified in 1100 and 1200) and the Mineral product tax (classified in 5121) should be classified in heading 6000 since under articles 72 and 519 of the Local Tax Law these taxes are regarded as levies on the business or mining activity itself.

Heading 2000: Includes some unidentifiable voluntary contributions.

Heading 2300: Includes contributions to the National pension, National Health Insurance and the Farmer's pension fund. Contributions to the Farmer's pension fund are not available for the years before 1999.

Heading 4100: Municipal property tax, includes Prefectural property tax from 1990 to 1994 because data are not available to provide a breakdown.

Heading 5121: Municipal tobacco tax, includes Prefectural tobacco tax from 1990 to 1994 because data are not available to provide a breakdown.

Heading 5121: In sub-item Petroleum and coal tax, the data before 2003 refer to petroleum tax.

Source: Tax Bureau, Ministry of Finance.

StatLink http://dx.doi.org/10.1787/888933428237

Table 4.3. Korea
Details of tax revenue

Billion KRW

	1997	2000	2007	2008	2009	2010	2011	2012	2013	2014
Total tax revenue	**102 916**	**136 295**	**258 571**	**272 201**	**273 647**	**295 968**	**321 915**	**341 336**	**347 332**	**365 428**
1000 Taxes on income, profits and capital gains	**26 916**	**39 254**	**82 239**	**84 321**	**77 897**	**82 905**	**96 845**	**101 944**	**101 792**	**106 353**
1100 Of individuals	16 543	19 950	43 276	40 910	38 618	42 098	47 299	51 185	53 311	59 457
Income tax	0	0	0	0	0	0	0	0	0	0
Dividends and interest income tax	0	0	4 682	4 659	4 762	4 425	4 896	5 152	4 889	4 628
Wages and salaries income tax	0	0	14 124	15 595	13 407	15 517	18 337	19 627	21 931	25 359
Other income tax	0	0	2 607	2 698	2 829	2 986	3 365	3 595	3 432	3 805
Global income tax	12 911	16 128	6 151	4 078	6 117	6 369	8 300	9 938	10 901	11 486
Defence tax on income tax	0	0	0	0	0	0	0	0	0	0
Education tax on income tax	0	0	0	0	0	0	0	0	0	0
Rural development tax on interest, bus. Inc. & cap.gains relief	149	156	160	148	199	179	156	125	124	115
Inhabitant tax on income tax (local)	1 526	2 285	4 260	4 407	3 996	4 459	4 856	5 293	5 377	6 017
1110 On income and profits	14 586	18 569	31 984	31 585	31 310	33 935	39 910	43 730	46 654	51 410
1120 On capital gains	1 957	1 381	11 292	9 325	7 308	8 163	7 389	7 455	6 657	8 047
Capital gains tax	1 957	1 381	11 292	9 325	7 308	8 163	7 389	7 455	6 657	8 047
1200 Corporate	10 158	19 271	38 963	43 409	39 279	40 807	49 546	50 759	48 481	46 896
Corporation tax - withholding	5 501	8 577	8 360	7 417	4 681	9 095	10 534	11 516	12 176	12 172
Corporation tax - final returns	3 924	9 302	27 057	31 737	30 570	28 173	34 339	34 416	31 679	30 478
Defence tax on corporation tax	0	0	0	0	0	0	0	0	0	0
Inhabitant tax on corporation tax (local)	733	1 142	3 152	3 756	3 556	3 094	3 953	4 258	4 118	3 882
Rural development tax corporate income	0	251	394	498	472	445	720	569	508	364
1210 On profits	10 158	19 271	38 963	43 409	39 279	40 807	49 546	50 759	48 481	46 896
Excess profit tax	0	0	0	0	0	0	0	0	0	0
1220 On capital gains	0	0	0	0	0	0	0	0	0	0
Capital gains tax	..	..	..	..	..	..	..	..	..	..
1300 Unallocable between 1100 and 1200	215	33	0	2	0	0	0	0	0	0
Business income tax	0	0	..	0	..	..	..	..	..	..
Real estate income tax	0	0	..	0	..	..	..	..	..	..
Defence tax on real estate & business income	0	0	..	0	..	..	..	..	..	..
Rural dev. tax on bus. inc. & cap. gains relief	211	30	..	2	..	..	..	..	..	..
Inhabitant tax before 1990 (local)	1	0	..	0	..	..	..	..	..	..
Farm land tax (local)	3	3	..	0	..	..	..	..	..	..
Inhabitant tax on farm land tax (local)	0	0	..	0	..	..	..	..	..	..
2000 Social security contributions	**14 583**	**22 759**	**53 588**	**59 415**	**63 939**	**69 090**	**77 234**	**84 380**	**91 596**	**98 184**
2100 Employees	6 376	8 578	21 773	24 236	25 638	28 213	31 875	35 670	38 396	41 355
Veterans' relief fund	0	0	0	0	0	0	0	0	0	0
Soldiers' annuity fund	0	0	0	0	0	0	0	0	0	0
Unemployment insurance	264	598	1 164	1 288	1 346	1 358	1 698	2 138	2 418	2 866
National welfare pension fund	3 597	4 325	9 338	9 976	10 358	11 004	11 832	12 867	13 890	14 823
Social benefit fund	0	0	0	0	0	0	0	0	0	0
Health insurance	1 149	2 066	8 180	9 702	10 581	11 783	13 954	15 718	17 128	18 492
Teachers' pensions	219	279	581	612	621	868	940	1 229	1 077	1 081
Government employees' pensions	1 013	1 144	2 202	2 345	2 308	2 878	3 106	3 345	3 435	3 593
Military personal pensions	134	166	308	313	313	322	345	373	448	500
2110 On a payroll basis	..	8 578	21 773	24 236	25 638	28 213	31 875	35 670	38 396	41 355
2120 On an income tax basis	..	0	0	0	0	0	0	0	0	0
2200 Employers	5 901	9 409	23 557	26 194	28 981	30 856	34 366	36 911	41 518	44 806
Ind. works' insurance fund	1 819	1 876	4 431	4 844	4 732	4 632	4 632	5 508	5 436	5 797
Soldiers' annuity fund	0	0	0	0	0	0	0	0	0	0
Pneumoconiosis fund	0	0	0	0	0	0	0	0	0	0
Unemployment insurance	653	1 449	2 474	2 681	2 843	2 860	3 347	4 166	4 545	5 150
Veterans' relief fund	0	0	0	0	0	0	0	0	0	0
National welfare pension fund	1 814	4 340	9 383	10 009	10 393	11 052	11 833	12 930	13 958	14 909
Social benefit fund	0	0	0	0	0	0	0	0	0	0
Health insurance	1 459	1 547	6 844	8 213	8 980	11 718	13 889	13 576	16 826	18 133
Teachers' pensions	156	197	425	447	456	594	665	731	753	0
Government employees' pensions	0	0	0	0	0	0	0	0	0	817
2210 On a payroll basis	..	9 409	23 557	26 194	28 981	30 856	34 366	36 911	41 518	44 806
2220 On an income tax basis	..	0	0	0	0	0	0	0	0	0
2300 Self-employed or non-employed	2 306	4 772	8 258	8 985	9 320	10 021	10 993	11 799	11 682	12 023
2310 On a payroll basis	0	0	0	0	0	0	0	0	0	0
2320 On an income tax basis	2 306	4 772	8 258	8 985	9 234	10 021	10 993	11 799	11 682	12 023
2400 Unallocable between 2100, 2200 and 2300	0	0	0	0	0	0	0	0	0	0
2410 On a payroll basis	..	..	..	..	..	..	..	..	..	..
2420 On an income tax basis	..	..	..	..	..	..	..	..	..	..

Table 4.3. Korea *(cont.)*
Details of tax revenue

Billion KRW

	1997	2000	2007	2008	2009	2010	2011	2012	2013	2014
3000 Taxes on payroll and workforce	**309**	**258**	**619**	**682**	**681**	**714**	**803**	**868**	**981**	**1 042**
Workshop tax on workforce (local)	309	258	619	682	681	714	803	868	981	1 042
Vocational training promotion fund	0	0	0	0	0	0	0	0	0	0
4000 Taxes on property	**13 088**	**16 846**	**33 109**	**32 468**	**31 803**	**33 516**	**36 555**	**36 213**	**35 847**	**40 305**
4100 Recurrent taxes on immovable property	2 986	3 385	9 196	9 859	8 859	9 270	9 779	10 315	10 809	11 654
Property tax (local)	577	728	3 755	4 411	4 423	4 817	7 617	8 049	8 267	8 780
City planning tax on urban real estate (local)	731	815	1 883	2 183	2 269	2 465	5	3	0	0
Community facilities tax (local)	268	341	543	589	591	650	705	766	912	1 138
Tax on excessive land holdings (local)	0	0	0	0	0	0	0	0	0	0
Tax on aggregate land holdings (local)	1 279	1 282	5	0	0	0	0	0	0	0
Rural dev. tax on local agg. land holdings tax	63	81	1	0	0	0	0	0	0	0
Tax on excessively increased land value	-1	0	0	0	0	0	0	0	0	0
Comprehensive real estate tax	0	0	2 414	2 130	1 207	1 029	1 102	1 131	1 224	1 307
Rural dev. tax on comprehensive real estate tax	0	0	483	428	242	208	223	228	250	265
4110 Households	0	0	0	0	0	0	0	0	0	0
4120 Others	68	138	112	118	127	101	127	138	156	164
Workshop tax on property (local)	68	138	112	118	127	101	127	138	156	164
4200 Recurrent taxes on net wealth	0	0	0	0	0	0	0	0	0	0
4210 Individual	..	..	..	..	..	..	..	..	..	..
4220 Corporate	..	..	..	..	..	..	..	..	..	..
4300 Estate, inheritance and gift taxes	1 161	989	2 842	2 777	2 431	3 076	3 333	4 021	4 290	4 625
4310 Estate and inheritance taxes	605	449	1 059	1 182	1 221	1 203	1 259	1 719	1 587	1 696
Inheritance tax	605	449	1 059	1 182	1 221	1 203	1 259	1 719	1 587	1 696
Defence tax on inheritance tax	0	0	0	0	0	0	0	0	0	0
4320 Gift taxes	556	540	1 783	1 595	1 210	1 873	2 074	2 302	2 703	2 929
Gift tax	556	540	1 783	1 595	1 210	1 873	2 074	2 302	2 703	2 929
Defence tax on gift tax	0	0	0	0	0	0	0	0	0	0
4400 Taxes on financial and capital transactions	8 774	11 935	21 071	19 832	20 513	21 170	23 443	21 877	20 748	24 026
Registration tax (local)	4 257	4 528	7 254	7 143	7 131	7 370	7 680	7 645	1 312	1 485
Registration tax	0	0	0	0	0	0	0	0	0	0
Defence tax on registration tax	0	0	0	0	0	0	0	0	0	0
Rural dev. tax on local acquisition tax	164	246	627	635	621	632	982	853	874	843
Rural dev. tax on local registration tax	211	66	143	142	169	144	2	2	1	1
Securities transactions tax	262	2 736	3 469	2 788	3 534	3 667	4 279	3 681	3 077	3 121
Rural dev. tax on securities transaction tax	170	823	1 729	1 635	1 870	2 010	2 515	1 769	1 529	1 459
Acquisition tax (local)	3 319	3 148	7 261	6 916	6 644	6 825	7 361	7 326	13 318	16 391
Stamp tax	390	388	588	573	544	522	624	601	637	726
4500 Non-recurrent taxes	167	537	0	0	0	0	0	0	0	0
Asset revaluation tax	167	537	..	..	..	..	..	..	..	..
4510 On net wealth	..	..	..	..	..	..	..	..	..	..
4520 Other non-recurrent taxes	..	..	..	..	..	..	..	..	..	..
4600 Other recurrent taxes on property	0	0	0	0	0	0	0	0	0	0
5000 Taxes on goods and services	**43 978**	**52 271**	**80 861**	**86 096**	**87 043**	**99 769**	**100 551**	**106 402**	**106 717**	**109 451**
5100 Taxes on production, sale, transfer, etc	41 699	50 023	78 414	83 412	84 135	96 573	93 983	99 731	99 970	102 531
5110 General taxes	19 488	23 212	40 942	43 820	46 992	51 800	54 868	58 702	59 105	62 975
5111 Value added taxes	19 488	23 212	40 942	43 820	46 992	51 800	54 868	58 702	59 105	62 975
Value added tax	19 488	23 212	40 942	43 820	46 992	51 800	54 868	58 702	59 105	62 975
5112 Sales tax	0	0	0	0	0	0	0	0	0	0
Business tax	..	..	..	..	..	..	..	..	..	..
5113 Other	0	0	0	0	0	0	0	0	0	0
5120 Taxes on specific goods and services	22 211	26 811	37 472	39 592	37 143	44 773	39 115	41 029	40 865	39 556

Table 4.3. Korea *(cont.)*
Details of tax revenue

Billion KRW

	1997	2000	2007	2008	2009	2010	2011	2012	2013	2014
5121 Excises	14 616	18 155	27 880	28 344	25 341	31 340	25 401	28 410	27 661	28 226
Commodity tax	0	0	0	0	0	0	0	0	0	0
Defence tax on commodity tax	0	0	0	0	0	0	0	0	0	0
Liquor tax	1 790	1 963	2 268	2 831	2 771	2 878	2 529	2 999	2 947	2 852
Defence tax on liquor tax	0	0	0	0	0	0	0	0	0	0
Education tax on liquor tax	418	516	580	739	713	724	644	774	764	728
Textile tax	0	0	0	0	0	0	0	0	0	0
Petroleum tax	0	0	0	0	0	0	0	0	0	0
Transport tax on petrol products	5 547	8 404	11 464	11 909	10 092	13 970	11 546	13 809	13 248	13 440
Education tax on transport tax	758	1 247	1 715	1 782	1 483	2 133	1 726	2 030	1 895	2 074
Electricity and gas tax	0	0	0	0	0	0	0	0	0	0
Special excise tax	3 036	2 985	5 161	4 499	3 642	5 066	5 537	5 336	5 484	5 624
Defence tax on special excise tax	0	0	0	0	0	0	0	0	0	0
Education tax on special excise tax	804	498	607	536	322	501	589	525	485	495
Rural development on special excise tax	26	37	54	47	20	24	45	56	56	60
Tobacco sales tax (local)	0	0	0	0	0	0	0	0	0	0
Tobacco consumption tax (local)	2 236	2 251	2 761	2 920	3 011	2 875	2 785	2 881	2 782	2 953
Motor fuel tax (local)	0	254	3 270	3 081	3 287	3 169	0	0	0	0
5122 Profits of fiscal monopolies	0	0	0	0	0	0	0	0	0	0
Monopoly profit	..	..	..	..	..	..	..	..	..	..
5123 Customs and import duties	5 941	5 936	7 690	9 068	9 486	11 046	11 350	10 220	11 012	9 132
Customs duties	5 798	5 800	7 411	8 776	9 169	10 666	10 990	9 816	10 562	8 721
Defence tax on customs duties	0	0	0	0	0	0	0	0	0	0
Special customs duties	0	0	0	0	0	0	0	0	0	0
Tonnage tax	0	0	0	0	0	0	0	0	0	0
Education tax on imports	116	99	234	246	273	336	322	375	429	390
Rural dev. tax on customs exemptions	27	37	45	46	44	44	38	29	21	21
Previous year receipts	0	0	0	0	0	0	0	0	0	0
5124 Taxes on exports	0	0	0	0	0	0	0	0	0	0
5125 Taxes on investment goods	0	0	0	0	0	0	0	0	0	0
5126 Taxes on specific services	1 654	2 720	1 902	2 180	2 316	2 387	2 364	2 399	2 192	2 198
Telephone tax	789	1 457	0	0	0	0	0	0	0	0
Defence tax on telephone tax	0	0	0	0	0	0	0	0	0	0
Entertainment tax	0	0	0	0	0	0	0	0	0	0
Defence tax on entertainment tax	0	0	0	0	0	0	0	0	0	0
Entertainment tax (local)	0	0	0	0	0	0	0	0	0	0
Travel tax	0	0	0	0	0	0	0	0	0	0
Admission tax	0	0	0	0	0	0	0	0	0	0
Defence tax on admission tax	0	0	0	0	0	0	0	0	0	0
Education tax on banking & insurance	369	473	721	872	964	951	966	932	938	920
Horse race tax (local)	361	566	864	989	1 002	1 068	1 072	1 129	1 042	1 073
Rural dev. tax on horse race tax	18	84	165	174	203	215	214	221	212	205
Butchery tax (local)	47	51	52	52	56	58	5	0	0	0
Regional development tax (local)	71	89	100	93	91	95	107	117	0	0
5127 Other taxes on internat. trade and transactions	0	0	0	0	0	0	0	0	0	0
5128 Other taxes	0	0	0	0	0	0	0	0	0	0
5130 Unallocable between 5110 and 5120	0	0	0	0	0	0	0	0	0	0
5200 Taxes on use of goods and to perform activities	2 279	2 248	2 447	2 684	2 908	3 196	6 568	6 671	6 747	6 920
5210 Recurrent taxes	2 279	2 248	2 447	2 684	2 908	3 196	6 568	6 671	6 747	6 920
Licence tax (local)	225	241	77	73	74	76	78	78	0	0
Automobile tax (local)	2 054	2 007	2 370	2 611	2 834	3 120	6 490	6 593	6 747	6 920
5211 Paid by households: motor vehicles	..	..	..	..	..	..	..	..	..	..
5212 Paid by others: motor vehicles	..	..	..	..	..	..	..	..	..	..
5213 Paid in respect of other goods	..	..	..	..	..	..	..	..	..	..
5220 Non-recurrent taxes	0	0	0	0	0	0	0	0	0	0
5300 Unallocable between 5100 and 5200	0	0	0	0	0	0	0	0	0	0
6000 Other taxes	**4 041**	**4 907**	**8 155**	**9 219**	**12 284**	**9 974**	**9 927**	**11 529**	**10 399**	**10 093**
6100 Paid solely by business	0	0	0	0	0	0	0	0	0	0
6200 Other	4 041	4 907	8 155	9 219	12 284	9 974	9 927	11 529	10 399	10 093
Unallocable tax revenue	0	0	0	0	0	0	0	0	0	0
Previous year tax	779	1 474	2 965	3 759	6 890	4 449	4 232	5 768	4 774	4 049
Previous year tax (local)	340	474	672	592	600	654	728	680	601	589
Unallocable defence tax	-8	-3	0	0	0	0	0	0	0	0
Education tax on local taxes	2 931	2 962	4 518	4 868	4 794	4 871	4 967	5 081	5 024	5 455

Note:

Year ending 31st December.

Data are on a cash basis.

Heading 2000: From 1997 the contributions to the three funds (civil servant pension fund, private school teachers' pension fund and medical insurance fund) are classified as security social contributions. The reasons for the change are that the contributions either became mandatory or the fund started to be managed by public authorities in that year, thereby meeting the OECD definition of social security contributions.

Heading 2200: From 2007, this includes long-term care insurance.

Source: Ministry of Finance and Economy, Ministry of Home Affairs.

StatLink http://dx.doi.org/10.1787/888933428249

Table 4.4. Malaysia
Details of tax revenue

Million MYR

	1997	2000	2007	2008	2009	2010	2011	2012	2013	2014
Total tax revenue	**56 905**	**51 857**	**102 668**	**120 909**	**114 754**	**118 302**	**144 297**	**161 539**	**166 269**	**175 452**
1000 Taxes on income, profits and capital gains	**27 648**	**27 339**	**65 671**	**79 032**	**75 269**	**75 058**	**98 018**	**111 676**	**114 113**	**120 284**
1100 Of individuals	6 429	7 015	11 661	14 966	15 590	17 805	20 203	22 977	23 055	24 423
1110 On income and profits	6 429	7 015	11 661	14 966	15 590	17 805	20 203	22 977	23 055	24 423
1120 On capital gains	0	0	0	0	0	0	0	0	0	0
1200 Corporate	20 552	19 923	52 615	62 041	57 725	55 156	74 653	85 239	87 949	92 223
1210 On profits	20 552	19 923	52 615	62 041	57 725	55 156	74 653	85 239	87 949	92 223
Company income tax	16 688	13 905	32 149	37 741	30 199	36 266	46 888	51 288	58 175	65 240
Petroleum income tax	3 861	6 010	20 453	24 191	27 231	18 713	27 748	33 934	29 753	26 956
Offshore business activity tax	3	8	13	17	15	15	17	18	20	27
Levy on electricity	0	0	0	92	280	162	0	0	1	0
1220 On capital gains	0	0	0	0	0	0	0	0	0	0
1300 Unallocable between 1100 and 1200	666	402	1 395	2 025	1 954	2 097	3 162	3 459	3 109	3 639
Cooperatives income tax	143	87	189	204	546	378	357	345	286	169
Withholding income tax	0	0	1 190	1 350	1 328	1 268	1 519	2 097	2 008	2 184
Other income tax	0	0	17	22	23	21	17	21	23	24
Real property gains tax	523	247	0	110	42	303	509	608	785	1 210
Exit levy	0	41	0	0	0	0	0	0	0	0
Windfall levy on crude palm oil	0	0	0	112	0	0	0	0	0	0
Windfall levy on crude palm kernel oil	0	26	0	27	0	0	0	0	0	0
Levy on fresh fruit bunch	0	0	0	199	16	127	761	388	7	51
2000 Social security contributions	**0**	**990**	**1 690**	**1 835**	**1 867**	**2 008**	**2 172**	**2 326**	**2 518**	**2 689**
2100 Employees	0	218	371	402	409	439	475	508	552	588
2110 On a payroll basis	..	218	371	402	409	439	475	508	552	588
2120 On an income tax basis	..	0	0	0	0	0	0	0	0	0
2200 Employers	0	772	1 319	1 433	1 458	1 569	1 697	1 818	1 966	2 101
2210 On a payroll basis	..	772	1 319	1 433	1 458	1 569	1 697	1 818	1 966	2 101
2220 On an income tax basis	..	0	0	0	0	0	0	0	0	0
2300 Self-employed or non-employed	0	0	0	0	0	0	0	0	0	0
2310 On a payroll basis	..	..	..	..	..	..	..	..	..	..
2320 On an income tax basis	..	..	..	..	..	..	..	..	..	..
2400 Unallocable between 2100, 2200 and 2300	0	0	0	0	0	0	0	0	0	0
2410 On a payroll basis	..	..	..	..	..	..	..	..	..	..
2420 On an income tax basis	..	..	..	..	..	..	..	..	..	..
3000 Taxes on payroll and workforce	**0**	**0**	**0**	**0**	**0**	**0**	**0**	**0**	**0**	**0**
4000 Taxes on property	**1 431**	**1 776**	**4 099**	**4 312**	**4 471**	**4 729**	**5 009**	**5 243**	**5 350**	**5 941**
4100 Recurrent taxes on immovable property	1 412	1 774	4 099	4 311	4 471	4 729	5 009	5 241	5 349	5 939
Quit rent	..	..	1 208	1 264	1 284	1 385	1 501	1 561	1 489	1 549
4110 Households	1 412	1 774	2 891	3 047	3 187	3 344	3 508	3 680	3 860	4 390
Assessment tax	1 412	1 774	2 891	3 047	3 187	3 344	3 508	3 680	3 860	4 390
4120 Others	0	0	0	0	0	0	0	0	0	0
4200 Recurrent taxes on net wealth	0	0	0	0	0	0	0	0	0	0
4210 Individual	..	..	..	..	..	..	..	..	..	..
4220 Corporate	..	..	..	..	..	..	..	..	..	..
4300 Estate, inheritance and gift taxes	19	2	0	1	0	0	0	2	1	2
4310 Estate and inheritance taxes	19	2	..	1	..	..	..	2	1	2
Estate duty	19	2	..	1	..	..	..	2	1	2
4320 Gift taxes	0	0	0	0	0	0	0	0	0	0
4400 Taxes on financial and capital transactions	0	0	0	0	0	0	0	0	0	0
4500 Non-recurrent taxes	0	0	0	0	0	0	0	0	0	0
4510 On net wealth	..	..	..	..	..	..	..	..	..	..
4520 Other non-recurrent taxes	..	..	..	..	..	..	..	..	..	..
4600 Other recurrent taxes on property	0	0	0	0	0	0	0	0	0	0
5000 Taxes on goods and services	**25 061**	**19 910**	**27 483**	**32 194**	**29 746**	**32 268**	**34 114**	**36 647**	**37 871**	**40 030**
5100 Taxes on production, sale, transfer, etc	23 195	17 990	25 772	30 323	27 834	30 218	31 883	34 317	35 421	37 411
5110 General taxes	6 167	5 968	6 642	8 374	8 603	8 171	8 577	9 496	10 068	10 939
5111 Value added taxes	0	0	0	0	0	0	0	0	0	0
5112 Sales tax	6 167	5 968	6 642	8 374	8 603	8 171	8 577	9 496	10 068	10 939
On local goods	4 160	3 894	4 178	4 986	5 348	4 886	4 995	5 358	5 626	6 130
On imported goods	2 008	2 074	2 464	3 387	3 255	3 285	3 583	4 138	4 442	4 809
5113 Other	0	0	0	0	0	0	0	0	0	0
5120 Taxes on specific goods and services	15 266	10 245	16 897	19 584	16 822	19 624	20 765	22 184	22 756	23 930
5121 Excise duties	6 053	3 803	8 990	10 682	10 068	11 770	11 517	12 187	12 193	12 925
On local goods	6 053	3 803	7 910	9 174	8 474	9 350	8 415	8 420	8 395	8 456
On imported goods	0	0	1 081	1 509	1 595	2 420	3 102	3 767	3 798	4 468
5122 Profits of fiscal monopolies	0	0	0	0	0	0	0	0	0	0
5123 Customs and import duties	6 524	3 599	2 424	2 635	2 114	1 966	2 026	2 282	2 524	2 670
5124 Taxes on exports	1 053	1 032	2 322	2 779	1 152	1 810	2 081	1 968	1 930	1 893

Table 4.4. Malaysia *(cont.)*
Details of tax revenue

Million MYR

	1997	2000	2007	2008	2009	2010	2011	2012	2013	2014
5125 Taxes on investment goods	0	0	0	0	0	0	0	0	0	0
5126 Taxes on specific services	1 475	1 701	3 013	3 345	3 344	3 926	4 982	5 583	5 944	6 278
Pool betting duties and sweepstakes	0	0	0	0	0	0	0	0	0	0
Service tax	1 475	1 701	3 013	3 345	3 344	3 926	4 982	5 583	5 944	6 278
5127 Other taxes on internat. trade and transactions	160	110	147	142	143	151	159	164	165	165
5128 Other taxes	0	0	0	0	0	0	0	0	0	0
5130 Unallocable between 5110 and 5120	1 761	1 777	2 233	2 365	2 409	2 423	2 541	2 638	2 597	2 542
5200 Taxes on use of goods and to perform activities	1 866	1 920	1 711	1 871	1 912	2 050	2 231	2 329	2 450	2 619
5210 Recurrent taxes	1 863	1 918	1 709	1 869	1 909	2 047	2 227	2 326	2 447	2 617
5211 Paid by households: motor vehicles	1 852	1 909	1 688	1 799	1 856	1 992	2 183	2 283	2 407	2 532
Motor vehicle licences	1 852	1 909	1 688	1 799	1 856	1 992	2 183	2 283	2 407	2 532
5212 Paid by others: motor vehicles	11	9	20	17	17	18	5	3	3	3
Commercial vehicle licences	11	9	19	16	16	17	5	3	3	3
Tour vehicle licences	0	0	1	1	1	1	1	0	0	0
5213 Paid in respect of other goods	0	0	0	53	36	38	39	39	37	81
Petroleum permits	0	0	0	1	1	1	1	1	0	4
Bank licences fees	0	0	0	53	35	37	38	39	37	78
5220 Non-recurrent taxes	3	2	3	2	2	2	4	3	2	2
Environment pollution licences	2	2	3	2	2	2	4	3	2	2
Film rental tax	1	0	0	0	0	0	0	0	0	0
5300 Unallocable between 5100 and 5200	0	0	0	0	0	0	0	0	0	0
6000 Other taxes	**2 764**	**1 841**	**3 725**	**3 537**	**3 401**	**4 240**	**4 984**	**5 648**	**6 417**	**6 508**
6100 Paid solely by business	0	0	0	0	0	0	0	0	0	0
6200 Other	2 764	1 841	3 725	3 537	3 401	4 240	4 984	5 648	6 417	6 508
Share transfer tax	0	0	0	0	0	0	0	0	0	0
Stamp duties	2 714	1 799	3 404	3 492	3 349	4 192	4 929	5 595	6 364	6 458
Other direct taxes	50	42	321	45	52	48	55	53	53	51

Note:

Year ending 31st December.

The data are on a cash basis.

Source: Ministry of Finance of Malaysia, Social Security Organisation, State Government Financial Report and Local Government Financial Report.

StatLink http://dx.doi.org/10.1787/888933428251

Table 4.5. Philippines
Details of tax revenue

Million PHP

	1997	2000	2007	2008	2009	2010	2011	2012	2013	2014
Total tax revenue	**447 976**	**564 343**	**1 121 594**	**1 254 204**	**1 205 348**	**1 330 768**	**1 469 547**	**1 669 306**	**1 868 601**	**2 111 568**
1000 Taxes on income, profits and capital gains	**164 170**	**217 798**	**453 338**	**511 128**	**467 706**	**521 707**	**612 432**	**691 232**	**767 819**	**840 680**
1100 Of individuals	59 749	83 006	141 673	150 936	137 108	167 605	194 025	223 165	246 894	283 873
1110 On income and profits	53 370	78 229	135 504	143 285	130 074	158 325	184 076	210 645	232 725	267 703
1120 On capital gains	6 379	4 777	6 170	7 651	7 033	9 280	9 949	12 520	14 169	16 170
1200 Corporate	95 449	116 980	282 504	328 484	303 391	326 967	392 400	432 850	486 898	523 183
1210 On profits	94 427	114 871	280 090	325 925	297 900	323 116	387 499	421 937	476 311	513 978
Other taxes on profits	1 022	2 110	2 414	2 559	5 492	3 851	4 902	10 913	10 587	9 205
1300 Unallocable between 1100 and 1200	8 973	17 812	29 160	31 707	27 207	27 135	26 007	35 217	34 027	33 624
2000 Social security contributions	**36 500**	**74 200**	**131 830**	**142 200**	**156 000**	**168 430**	**186 203**	**215 356**	**236 575**	**284 360**
2100 Employees	..	..	..	..	..	..	..	..	..	..
2110 On a payroll basis	..	..	..	..	..	..	..	..	..	..
2120 On an income tax basis	..	..	..	..	..	..	..	..	..	..
2200 Employers	2 800	19 900	26 520	27 700	33 000	34 300	38 008	54 215	54 662	80 130
2210 On a payroll basis	..	..	..	..	..	..	..	..	..	..
2220 On an income tax basis	..	..	..	..	..	..	..	..	..	..
2300 Self-employed or non-employed	..	..	..	..	..	..	..	..	..	..
2310 On a payroll basis	..	..	..	..	..	..	..	..	..	..
2320 On an income tax basis	..	..	..	..	..	..	..	..	..	..
2400 Unallocable between 2100, 2200 and 2300	33 700	54 300	105 310	114 500	123 000	134 130	148 195	161 141	181 913	204 230
2410 On a payroll basis	..	..	..	..	..	..	..	..	..	..
2420 On an income tax basis	..	..	..	..	..	..	..	..	..	..
3000 Taxes on payroll and workforce	**0**	**0**	**0**	**0**	**0**	**0**	**0**	**0**	**0**	**0**
4000 Taxes on property	**4 178**	**17 401**	**32 354**	**33 804**	**36 963**	**39 070**	**44 590**	**50 943**	**56 269**	**60 026**
4100 Recurrent taxes on immovable property	0	14 947	27 387	29 799	31 518	31 876	36 043	39 315	41 191	45 458
Real property tax (local government)	..	14 947	27 387	29 799	31 518	31 876	36 043	39 315	41 191	45 458
4110 Households	..	..	..	..	..	..	..	..	..	..
4120 Others	..	..	..	..	..	..	..	..	..	..
4200 Recurrent taxes on net wealth	0	0	0	0	0	0	0	0	0	0
4210 Individual	..	..	..	..	..	..	..	..	..	..
4220 Corporate	..	..	..	..	..	..	..	..	..	..
4300 Estate, inheritance and gift taxes	881	480	962	1 279	1 426	1 981	2 400	3 626	3 275	5 450
4310 Estate and inheritance taxes	677	302	650	855	982	1 451	1 635	2 315	1 650	3 489
4320 Gift taxes	204	178	312	424	444	531	765	1 312	1 625	1 960
4400 Taxes on financial and capital transactions	3 297	1 974	4 005	2 727	4 019	5 213	6 147	8 002	11 803	9 118
Stock transactions (RA 7717)	3 297	1 974	4 005	2 727	4 019	5 213	6 147	8 002	11 803	9 118
4500 Non-recurrent taxes	0	0	0	0	0	0	0	0	0	0
4510 On net wealth	..	..	..	..	..	..	..	..	..	..
4520 Other non-recurrent taxes	..	..	..	..	..	..	..	..	..	..
4600 Other recurrent taxes on property	0	0	0	0	0	0	0	0	0	0
5000 Taxes on goods and services	**225 025**	**237 243**	**456 497**	**510 474**	**498 883**	**549 890**	**568 870**	**648 504**	**735 896**	**844 442**
5100 Taxes on production, sale, transfer, etc	222 627	234 202	448 164	501 894	489 850	540 595	558 770	638 148	724 888	832 656
5110 General taxes	47 273	53 879	145 013	140 318	168 294	173 284	183 082	229 594	250 149	278 794
5111 Value added taxes	47 273	53 879	145 013	140 318	168 294	173 284	183 082	229 594	250 149	278 794
5112 Sales tax	0	0	0	0	0	0	0	0	0	0
5113 Other	0	0	0	0	0	0	0	0	0	0
5120 Taxes on specific goods and services	175 354	180 323	303 151	361 575	321 556	367 312	375 687	408 554	474 739	553 862
5121 Excises	63 048	61 677	54 998	61 415	60 548	67 203	67 993	72 346	118 856	135 315
Alcohol products	13 412	12 997	18 786	19 839	20 637	21 781	22 873	23 896	33 535	37 525
Tobacco products	16 027	17 427	23 206	27 561	24 236	31 730	25 997	32 942	71 608	82 725
Petroleum products	29 272	28 297	10 036	11 380	12 772	9 832	9 963	10 159	8 503	9 419
Automobiles	0	0	0	0	0	0	2 026	2 935	2 542	2 636
Mineral products	77	243	942	660	719	1 306	6 986	2 206	2 494	2 814
Others	4 259	2 712	2 028	1 976	2 183	2 555	148	208	174	196
5122 Profits of fiscal monopolies	0	0	0	0	0	0	0	0	0	0
5123 Customs and import duties	94 800	95 006	209 439	260 248	220 307	259 241	265 108	289 866	304 925	369 277
5124 Taxes on exports	0	0	0	0	0	0	0	0	0	0
5125 Taxes on investment goods	0	0	0	0	0	0	0	0	0	0
5126 Taxes on specific services	17 506	23 639	38 714	39 912	40 701	40 868	42 587	46 342	50 958	49 270
Banks and financial institutions	9 696	9 538	19 434	21 086	21 937	22 857	23 514	25 338	30 199	26 677
Travel tax (CHED/NCAA)	386	1 043	1 581	1 779	1 843	1 512	1 660	1 709	1 885	1 827
Immigration tax (BID)	18	47	42	46	39	59	61	64	69	72
Others	7 406	13 011	17 657	17 001	16 882	16 440	17 351	19 231	18 805	20 694
5127 Other taxes on internat. trade and transactions	0	0	0	0	0	0	0	0	0	0
5128 Other taxes	0	0	0	0	0	0	0	0	0	0
5130 Unallocable between 5110 and 5120	0	0	0	0	0	0	0	0	0	0
5200 Taxes on use of goods and perform activities	2 398	3 041	8 333	8 580	9 033	9 295	10 100	10 356	11 008	11 786

Table 4.5. Philippines *(cont.)*
Details of tax revenue

Million PHP

	1997	2000	2007	2008	2009	2010	2011	2012	2013	2014
5210 Recurrent taxes	2 398	3 041	8 333	8 580	9 033	9 295	10 100	10 356	11 008	11 786
LTO-Motor vehicle users' tax	2 398	3 041	8 333	8 580	9 033	9 295	10 100	10 356	11 008	11 786
5211 Paid by households: motor vehicles	..	..	..	..	..	..	..	..	..	..
5212 Paid by others: motor vehicles	..	..	..	..	..	..	..	..	..	..
5213 Paid in respect of other goods	0	0	0	0	0	0	0	0	0	0
5220 Non-recurrent taxes	0	0	0	0	0	0	0	0	0	0
5300 Unallocable between 5100 and 5200	0	0	0	0	0	0	0	0	0	0
6000 Other taxes	**18 103**	**17 702**	**47 575**	**56 598**	**45 797**	**51 671**	**57 452**	**63 271**	**72 042**	**82 060**
6100 Paid solely by business	0	0	0	0	0	0	0	0	0	0
6200 Other	18 103	17 702	47 575	56 598	45 797	51 671	57 452	63 271	72 042	82 060
Documentary stamp tax	16 477	16 170	35 147	40 054	37 484	42 629	47 879	52 455	60 356	69 036
DENR-Forest charges	116	175	164	147	132	239	150	204	132	133
Miscellaneous taxes	1 510	1 356	8 944	12 261	4 317	4 391	4 724	5 788	5 874	6 051
Other taxes (local government)	0	0	3 319	4 136	3 864	4 412	4 700	4 823	5 679	6 840

Note:

Year ending 31st December.

The data are on a cash basis.

Source: Department of Finance of the Philippines.

StatLink http://dx.doi.org/10.1787/888933428264

Table 4.6. Singapore
Details of tax revenue

Million SGD

	1997	2000	2007	2008	2009	2010	2011	2012	2013	2014
Total tax revenue	..	**25 627**	**36 630**	**37 709**	**36 616**	**41 848**	**46 076**	**50 118**	**51 146**	**54 110**
1000 Taxes on income, profits and capital gains	..	**13 538**	**16 621**	**19 286**	**17 211**	**18 687**	**20 579**	**22 411**	**22 050**	**23 940**
1100 Of individuals	..	3 543	4 537	5 414	6 114	6 470	6 871	7 714	7 688	8 927
1110 On income and profits	..	3 543	4 537	5 414	6 114	6 470	6 871	7 714	7 688	8 927
1120 On capital gains	..	0	0	0	0	0	0	0	0	0
1200 Corporate	..	9 509	10 934	12 696	9 961	11 260	12 450	13 360	13 209	13 887
1210 On profits	..	9 509	10 934	12 696	9 961	11 260	12 450	13 360	13 209	13 887
From corporate profits	..	8 316	9 250	10 554	9 551	10 687	12 096	12 821	12 680	13 372
Statutory board contributions	..	1 192	1 683	2 143	410	573	353	539	530	516
1220 On capital gains	..	0	0	0	0	0	0	0	0	0
1300 Unallocable between 1100 and 1200	..	486	1 150	1 176	1 137	957	1 258	1 337	1 152	1 126
Withholding taxes	..	486	1 150	1 176	1 137	957	1 258	1 337	1 152	1 126
2000 Social security contributions	..	**0**	**0**	**0**	**0**	**0**	**0**	**0**	**0**	**0**
2100 Employees	..	..	..	..	..	..	..	..	..	..
2110 On a payroll basis	..	..	..	..	..	..	..	..	..	..
2120 On an income tax basis	..	..	..	..	..	..	..	..	..	..
2200 Employers	..	..	..	..	..	..	..	..	..	..
2210 On a payroll basis	..	..	..	..	..	..	..	..	..	..
2220 On an income tax basis	..	..	..	..	..	..	..	..	..	..
2300 Self-employed or non-employed	..	..	..	..	..	..	..	..	..	..
2310 On a payroll basis	..	..	..	..	..	..	..	..	..	..
2320 On an income tax basis	..	..	..	..	..	..	..	..	..	..
2400 Unallocable between 2100, 2200 and 2300	..	..	..	..	..	..	..	..	..	..
2410 On a payroll basis	..	..	..	..	..	..	..	..	..	..
2420 On an income tax basis	..	..	..	..	..	..	..	..	..	..
3000 Taxes on payroll and workforce	..	**0**	**0**	**0**	**0**	**0**	**0**	**0**	**0**	**0**
4000 Taxes on property	..	**2 863**	**6 259**	**4 335**	**4 374**	**6 080**	**7 077**	**8 078**	**8 112**	**7 124**
4100 Recurrent taxes on immovable property	..	1 535	2 428	2 856	1 979	2 798	3 899	3 760	4 179	4 340
4110 Households	..	..	..	..	..	..	..	..	..	..
4120 Others	..	..	..	..	..	..	..	..	..	..
4200 Recurrent taxes on net wealth	..	0	0	0	0	0	0	0	0	0
4210 Individual	..	..	..	..	..	..	..	..	..	..
4220 Corporate	..	..	..	..	..	..	..	..	..	..
4300 Estate, inheritance and gift taxes	..	71	154	47	8	5	3	8	3	1
4310 Estate and inheritance taxes	..	71	154	47	8	5	3	8	3	1
4320 Gift taxes	..	0	0	0	0	0	0	0	0	0
4400 Taxes on financial and capital transactions	..	1 257	3 677	1 432	2 386	3 277	3 175	4 310	3 930	2 784
4500 Non-recurrent taxes	..	0	0	0	0	0	0	0	0	0
4510 On net wealth	..	..	..	..	..	..	..	..	..	..
4520 Other non-recurrent taxes	..	..	..	..	..	..	..	..	..	..
4600 Other recurrent taxes on property	..	0	0	0	0	0	0	0	0	0
5000 Taxes on goods and services	..	**7 967**	**12 053**	**12 158**	**12 622**	**14 376**	**15 113**	**15 287**	**15 736**	**16 949**
5100 Taxes on production, sale, transfer, etc	..	5 462	9 864	10 323	10 766	12 525	13 193	13 485	14 081	15 346
5110 General taxes	..	2 121	6 165	6 487	6 914	8 198	8 687	9 038	9 513	10 215
5111 Value added taxes	..	2 121	6 165	6 487	6 914	8 198	8 687	9 038	9 513	10 215
5112 Sales tax	..	0	0	0	0	0	0	0	0	0
5113 Other	..	0	0	0	0	0	0	0	0	0
5120 Taxes on specific goods and services	..	3 341	3 699	3 836	3 852	4 327	4 506	4 447	4 568	5 131
5121 Excises	..	1 847	1 985	2 065	2 125	2 049	2 133	2 142	2 189	2 540
Liquors	..	..	414	415	433	470	496	517	518	634
Tobacco	..	..	700	794	932	889	967	969	1 043	1 228
Petroleum Products	..	..	386	398	413	419	416	415	414	419
Motor Vehicles	..	..	483	456	344	267	248	233	206	251
Compressed Natural Gas Unit Duty	..	..	..	..	..	..	1	3	3	3
Others	..	..	3	4	4	5	5	5	5	6
5122 Profits of fiscal monopolies	..	0	0	0	0	0	0	0	0	0
5123 Customs and import duties	..	..	..	..	..	..	..	..	..	..
5124 Taxes on exports	..	0	0	0	0	0	0	0	0	0
5125 Taxes on investment goods	..	0	0	0	0	0	0	0	0	0
5126 Taxes on specific services	..	1 494	1 714	1 771	1 727	2 279	2 373	2 305	2 379	2 591
Betting duty	..	1 494	1 714	1 771	1 727	2 279	2 373	2 305	2 379	2 591
5127 Other taxes on internat. trade and transactions	..	0	0	0	0	0	0	0	0	0
5128 Other taxes	..	0	0	0	0	0	0	0	0	0
5130 Unallocable between 5110 and 5120	..	0	0	0	0	0	0	0	0	0
5200 Taxes on use of goods and perform activities	..	2 506	2 189	1 835	1 856	1 851	1 920	1 803	1 655	1 603
5210 Recurrent taxes	..	..	..	..	..	..	..	..	..	..
5211 Paid by households: motor vehicles	..	..	..	..	..	..	..	..	..	..
5212 Paid by others: motor vehicles	..	..	..	..	..	..	..	..	..	..

Table 4.6. Singapore *(cont.)*
Details of tax revenue

Million SGD

	1997	2000	2007	2008	2009	2010	2011	2012	2013	2014
5213 Paid in respect of other goods	..	..	..	..	..	..	..	..	..	..
5220 Non-recurrent taxes	..	..	..	..	..	..	..	..	..	..
5300 Unallocable between 5100 and 5200	..	0	0	0	0	0	0	0	0	0
6000 Other taxes	..	**1 259**	**1 698**	**1 930**	**2 410**	**2 706**	**3 307**	**4 342**	**5 248**	**6 097**
6100 Paid solely by business	..	0	0	0	0	0	0	0	0	0
6200 Other	..	1 259	1 698	1 930	2 410	2 706	3 307	4 342	5 248	6 097

Note:

Data are on a fiscal year basis ending 31st March. For example, the data for 2014 represent 1 April 2014 to 31 March 2015.

The data are on a cash basis.

There are no social security contributions in Singapore (heading 2000).

Recurrent taxes on immovable property (heading 4100) includes tax levied on all private properties, as well as properties owned by statutory boards.

Excises (heading 5121) comprises excises, customs and import duties.

Source: Ministry of Finance of Singapore.

StatLink http://dx.doi.org/10.1787/888933428270

ANNEX A

The OECD Interpretative Guide[1]

Table of contents

A.1. The OECD classification of taxes

1000 *Taxes on income, profits and capital gains*

- 1100 Taxes on income, profits and capital gains of individuals
  - 1110 On income and profits
  - 1120 On capital gains
- 1200 Corporate taxes on income, profits and capital gains
  - 1210 on income and profits
  - 1220 On capital gains
- 1300 Unallocable as between 1100 and 1200

2000 *Social security contributions*

- 2100 Employees
  - 2110 On a payroll basis
  - 2120 On an income tax basis
- 2200 Employers
  - 2210 On a payroll basis
  - 2220 On an income tax basis
- 2300 Self-employed, non-employed
  - 2310 On a payroll basis
  - 2320 On an income tax basis
- 2400 Unallocable as between 2100, 2200 and 2300
  - 2410 On a payroll basis
  - 2420 On an income tax basis

3000 *Taxes on payroll and workforce*

4000 *Taxes on property*

- 4100 Recurrent taxes on immovable property
  - 4110 Households
  - 4120 Other
- 4200 Recurrent taxes on net wealth
  - 4210 Individual
  - 4220 Corporate
- 4300 Estate, inheritance and gift taxes
  - 4310 Estate and inheritance taxes
  - 4320 Gift taxes
- 4400 Taxes on financial and capital transactions

4500 Other non-recurrent taxes on property

4510 On net wealth

4520 Other non-recurrent taxes

4600 Other recurrent taxes on property

5000 *Taxes on goods and services*

5100 Taxes on production, sale, transfer, leasing and delivery of goods and rendering of services

5110 General taxes

5111 Value-added taxes

5112 Sales taxes

5113 Other general taxes on goods and services

5120 Taxes on specific goods and services

5121 Excises

5122 Profits of fiscal monopolies

5123 Customs and import duties

5124 Taxes on exports

5125 Taxes on investment goods

5126 Taxes on specific services

5127 Other taxes on international trade and transactions

5128 Other taxes on specific goods and services

5130 Unallocable as between 5110 and 5120

5200 Taxes on use of goods, or on permission to use goods or perform activities

5210 Recurrent taxes

5211 Paid by households in respect of motor vehicles

5212 Paid by others in respect of motor vehicles

5213 Other recurrent taxes

5220 Non-recurrent taxes

5300 Unallocable as between 5100 and 5200

6000 *Other taxes*

6100 Paid solely by business

6200 Paid by other than business, or unidentifiable

The OECD Interpretative Guide[1]

A.2. Coverage

General criteria

1. In the OECD classification the term "taxes" is confined to compulsory unrequited payments to general government. Taxes are unrequited in the sense that benefits provided by government to taxpayers are not normally in proportion to their payments.

2. The term 'tax' does not include fines, penalties and compulsory loans paid to government. Borderline cases between tax and non-tax revenues in relation to certain fees and charges are discussed in §9–12.

3. General government consists of the central administration, agencies whose operations are under its effective control, state and local governments and their administrations, certain social security schemes and autonomous governmental entities, excluding public enterprises. This definition of government follows that of the 2008 System of National Accounts (SNA).[2] In that publication, the general government sector and its sub-sectors are defined in chapter 4, section F, pages 80-84.

4. Compulsory payments to supra-national bodies and their agencies are no longer included as taxes as from 1998, with some exceptions. However, custom duties collected by EU member states on behalf of the European Union are still identified as memorandum items and included in overall tax revenue amounts in the country tables (Chapter 4) of the country in which they are collected. (See §94). In countries where the church forms part of general government church taxes are included, provided they meet the criteria set out in §1 above. As the data refer to receipts of general government, levies paid to non-government bodies, welfare agencies or social insurance schemes outside general government, trade unions or trade associations, even where such levies are compulsory, are excluded. Compulsory payments to general government earmarked for such bodies are, however, included, provided that the government is not simply acting in an agency capacity.[3] Profits from fiscal monopolies are distinguished from those of other public enterprises and are treated as taxes because they reflect the exercise of the taxing power of the state by the use of monopoly powers (see §61–63), as are profits received by the government from the purchase and sale of foreign exchange at different rates (see §69).

5. Taxes paid by governments (e.g., social security contributions and payroll taxes paid by governments in their capacity as an employer, consumption taxes on their purchases or taxes on their property) are not excluded from the data provided. However, where it is possible to identify the amounts of revenue involved,[4] they are shown in Chapter 4.3 of this Report.

6. The relationship between this classification and that of the System of National Accounts (SNA) is set out in Sections A.9 and A.11 below. Because of the differences between the two classifications, the data shown in national accounts are sometimes calculated or classified differently from the practice set out in this guide. These and other differences are mentioned where appropriate (e.g., in §25 below) but it is not possible to refer to all of them. There may also be some differences between this classification and that employed domestically by certain national administrations (e.g., see §10 below), so that OECD and national statistics data may not always be consistent: any such differences, however, are likely to be very slight in terms of amounts of revenues involved.

Social security contributions

7. Compulsory social security contributions, as defined in §34 below, paid to general government, are treated here as tax revenues. Being compulsory payments to general government they clearly resemble taxes. They may, however, differ from other taxes in that the receipt of social security benefits depends, in most countries, upon appropriate contributions having been made, although the size of the benefits is not necessarily related to the amount of the contributions. Better comparability between countries is obtained by treating social security contributions as taxes, but they are listed under a separate heading so that they can be distinguished in any analysis.

8. Social security contributions which are either voluntary or not payable to general government (see §1) are not treated as taxes, though in some countries, as indicated in the country footnotes, there are difficulties in eliminating voluntary contributions and certain compulsory payments to the private sector. Imputed social security contributions are also not treated as taxes.

Fees, user charges and licence fees

9. Apart from vehicle licence fees, which are universally regarded as taxes, it is not easy to distinguish between those fees and user charges which are to be treated as taxes and those which are not, since, whilst a fee or charge is levied in connection with a specific service or activity, the strength of the link between the fee and the service provided may vary considerably, as may the relation between the amount of the fee and the cost of providing the service. Where the recipient of a service pays a fee clearly related to the cost of providing the service, the levy may be regarded as requited and under the definition of §1 would not be considered as a tax. In the following cases, however, a levy could be considered as 'unrequited':

a) where the charge greatly exceeds the cost of providing the service;

b) where the payer of the levy is not the receiver of the benefit (e.g. a fee collected from slaughterhouses to finance a service which is provided to farmers);

c) where government is not providing a specific service in return for the levy which it receives even though a licence may be issued to the payer (e.g. where the government grants a hunting, fishing or shooting licence which is not accompanied by the right to use a specific area of government land);

d) where benefits are received only by those paying the levy but the benefits received by each individual are not necessarily in proportion to his payments (e.g. a milk marketing levy paid by dairy farmers and used to promote the consumption of milk).

10. In marginal cases, however, the application of the criteria set out in §1 can be particularly difficult. The solution adopted – given the desirability of international uniformity and the relatively small amounts of revenue usually involved – is to follow the predominant practice among tax administrations rather than to allow each country to adopt its own view as to whether such levies are regarded as taxes or as non-tax revenue.[5]

11. A list of the main fees and charges in question and their normal[6] treatment in this publication is as follows:

Non-tax revenues: court fees; driving licence fees; harbour fees; passport fees; radio and television licence fees where public authorities provide the service.

Taxes within heading 5200:	permission to perform such activities as distributing films; hunting, fishing and shooting; providing entertainment or gambling facilities; selling alcohol or tobacco; permission to own dogs or to use or own motor vehicles or guns; severance taxes.

12. In practice it may not always be possible to isolate tax receipts from non-tax revenue receipts when they are recorded together. If it is estimated that the bulk of the receipts derive from non-tax revenues, the whole amount involved is treated as a non-tax revenue; otherwise, such government receipts are included and classified according to the rules provided in §27 below.

Royalties

13. Royalty payments for the right to extract oil and gas or to exploit other mineral resources are normally regarded as non-tax revenues since they are property income from government-owned land or resources.

Fines and penalties

14. In principle, fines and penalties charged on overdue taxes or penalties imposed for the attempted evasion of taxes should not be recorded as tax revenues. However it may not be possible to separate payments of fines or other penalties from the revenues from the taxes to which they relate. In this case the fines and penalties relating to a particular tax are recorded together with the revenues from that tax and fines and penalties paid with revenue from unidentifiable taxes are classified as other taxes in Category 6000. Fines not relating to tax offences (e.g. for parking offences), or not identifiable as relating to tax offences, are also not treated as tax revenues.

A.3. Basis of reporting

Accrual reporting

15. The data reported in this publication for recent years are predominantly recorded on an accrual basis, i.e. recorded at the time that the tax liability was created. Further information is provided in the footnotes to the country table in Chapter 4 of the Report.

16. However, data for earlier years are still predominantly recorded on a cash basis, i.e. at the time at which the payment was received by government. Thus, for example, taxes withheld by employers in one year but paid to the government in the following year and taxes due in one year but actually paid in the following year are both included in the receipts of the second year. Corrective transactions, such as refunds, repayments and drawbacks, are deducted from gross revenues of the period in which they are made.

17. Data on tax revenues are recorded without offsets for the administrative expenses connected with tax collection. Similarly, where the proceeds of tax are used to subsidise particular members of the community, the subsidy is not deducted from the yield of the tax, though the tax may be shown net of subsidies in the national records of some countries.

18. As regards fiscal monopolies (heading 5122), only the amount actually transferred to the government is included in government revenues. However, if any expenditures of fiscal monopolies are considered to be government expenditures (e.g. social expenditures undertaken by fiscal monopolies at the direction of the government) they are added back for the purpose of arriving at tax revenue figures (see §61 below).

The distinction between tax and expenditure provisions[7]

19. Because this publication is concerned only with the revenue side of government operations, no account being taken of the expenditure side, a distinction has to be made between tax and expenditure provisions. Normally there is no difficulty in making this distinction as expenditures are made outside the tax system and the tax accounts and under legislation separate from the tax legislation. In borderline cases, cash flow is used to distinguish between tax provisions and expenditure provisions. Insofar as a provision affects the flow of tax payments from the taxpayer to the government, it is regarded as a tax provision and is taken into account in the data shown in this publication. A provision which does not affect this flow is seen as an expenditure provision and is disregarded in the data recorded in this publication.

20. Tax allowances, exemptions and deductions against the tax base clearly affect the amount of tax paid to the government and are therefore considered as tax provisions. At the other extreme, those subsidies which cannot be offset against tax liability and which are clearly not connected with the assessment process, do not reduce tax revenues as recorded in this publication. Tax credits are amounts deductible from tax payable (as distinct from deductions from the tax base). Two types of tax credits are distinguished, those (referred to here as wastable tax credits) which are limited to the amount of the tax liability and therefore cannot give rise to a payment by the authorities to the taxpayer, and those (referred to as non-wastable tax credits) which are not so limited, so that the excess of the credit over the tax liability can be paid to the taxpayer.[8] A wastable tax credit, like a tax allowance, clearly affects the amount of tax paid to the government, and is therefore considered as a tax provision. The practice followed for non-wastable tax credits[9] is to distinguish between the 'tax expenditure component',[10] which is that portion of the credit that is used to reduce or eliminate a taxpayer's liability, and the 'transfer component', which is the portion that exceeds the taxpayer's liability and is paid to that taxpayer. Reported tax revenues should be reduced by the amount of the tax expenditure component but not by the amount of the transfer component. In addition, the amounts of the tax expenditure and transfer components should be reported as memorandum items in the country tables. Countries that are unable to distinguish between the tax expenditure and transfer components should indicate whether or not the tax revenues have been reduced by the total of these components, and provide any available estimates of the amounts of the two components. Further information is given in Chapter 2 of the Report, which illustrates the effect of alternative treatments of non-wastable tax credits on Tax to GDP.

Calendar and fiscal years

21. National authorities whose fiscal years do not correspond to the calendar year show data, where possible, on a calendar year basis to permit maximum comparability with the data of other countries. There remain a few countries where data refer to fiscal years. For these the GDP data used in the comparative tables also correspond to the fiscal years.

A.4. General classification criteria

The main classification criteria

22. The classification of receipts among the main headings (1000, 2000, 3000, 4000, 5000 and 6000) is generally governed by the base on which the tax is levied: 1000 income, profits and capital gains; 2000 and 3000 earnings, payroll or number of employees; 4000 property; 5000 goods and services; 6000 multiple bases, other bases or unidentifiable bases. Where a tax is calculated on more than one base, the receipts are, where possible, split among the various headings (see §27 and §77). The headings 4000 and 5000 cover

not only taxes where the tax base is the property, goods or services themselves but also certain related taxes. Thus, taxes on the transfer of property are included in 4400[11] and taxes on the use of goods or on permission to perform activities in 5200. In headings 4000 and 5000 a distinction is made in certain sub-headings between recurrent and non-recurrent taxes: recurrent taxes are defined as those levied at regular intervals (usually annually) and non-recurrent taxes are levied once and for all (see also §42 to §45, §48, §49 and §75 for particular applications of this distinction).

23. Earmarking of a tax for specific purposes does not affect the classification of tax receipts. However, as explained in §34 on the classification of social security contributions, the conferment of an entitlement to social benefits is crucial to the definition of the 2000 main heading.

24. The way that a tax is levied or collected (e.g. by use of stamps) does not affect classification.

Classification of taxpayers

25. In certain sub-headings distinctions are made between different categories of taxpayers. These distinctions vary from tax to tax:

a) Between individuals and corporations in relation to income and net wealth taxes

The basic distinction is that corporation income taxes, as distinct from individual income taxes, are levied on the corporation as an entity, not on the individuals who own it, and without regard to the personal circumstances of these individuals. The same distinction applies to net wealth taxes on corporations and those on individuals. Taxes paid on the profits of partnerships and the income of institutions, such as life insurance or pension funds, are classified according to the same rule. They are classified as corporate taxes (1200) if they are charged on the partnership or institution as an entity without regard to the personal circumstances of the owners. Otherwise, they are treated as individual taxes (1100). Usually, there is different legislation for the corporation taxes and for the individual taxes.[12] The distinction made here between individuals and corporations does not follow the sector classification between households, enterprises, and so on of the System of National Accounts for income and outlay accounts. The SNA classification requires certain unincorporated businesses[13] to be excluded from the household sector and included with non-financial enterprises and financial institutions. The tax on the profits of these businesses, however, cannot always be separated from the tax on the other income of their owners, or can be separated only on an arbitrary basis. No attempt at this separation is made here and the whole of the individual income tax is shown together without regard to the nature of the income chargeable.

b) Between households and others in relation to taxes on immovable property

Here the distinction is that adopted by the SNA for the production and consumption expenditure accounts. The distinction is between households as consumers (i.e. excluding non-incorporated business) on the one hand and producers on the other hand. However, taxes on dwellings occupied by households, whether paid by owner-occupiers, tenants or landlords, are classified under households. This follows the common distinction made between taxes on domestic property versus taxes on business property. Some countries are not, however, in a position to make this distinction.

c) Between households and others in relation to motor vehicle licences

Here the distinction is between households as consumers on the one hand and producers on the other, as in the production and consumption expenditure accounts of the SNA.

d) Between business and others in relation to the residual taxes (6000)

The distinction is the same as in c) above between producers on the one hand and households as consumers on the other hand. Taxes which are included under the heading 6000 because they involve more than one tax base or because the tax base does not fall within any of the previous categories but which are identifiable as levyable only on producers and not on households are included under 'business'. The rest of the taxes which are included under the heading 6000 are shown as 'other' or non-identified.

Surcharges

26. Receipts from surcharges in respect of particular taxes are usually classified with the receipts from the relevant tax whether or not the surcharge is temporary. If, however, the surcharge has a characteristic which would render it classifiable in a different heading of the OECD list, receipts from the surcharge are classified under that heading separately from the relevant tax.

Unidentifiable tax receipts and residual sub-headings

27. A number of cases arise where taxes cannot be identified as belonging entirely to a heading or sub-heading of the OECD classification and the following practices are applied in such cases:

a) The heading is known, but it is not known how receipts should be allocated between sub-headings: receipts are classified in the appropriate residual sub-heading (1300, 2400, 4520, 4600, 5130, 5300 or 6200).

b) It is known that the bulk of receipts from a group of taxes (usually local taxes) is derived from taxes within a particular heading or sub-heading, but some of the taxes in the group whose amount cannot be precisely ascertained may be classifiable in other headings or sub-headings: receipts are shown in the heading or sub-heading under which most of the receipts fall.

c) Neither the heading nor sub-heading of a tax (usually local) can be identified: the tax is classified in 6200 unless it is known that it is a tax on business in which case it is classified in 6100.

A.5. Commentaries on items of the list

1000 – *Taxes on income, profits and capital gains*

28. This heading covers taxes levied on the net income or profits (i.e. gross income minus allowable tax reliefs) of individuals and enterprises. Also covered are taxes levied on the capital gains of individuals and enterprises, and gains from gambling.

29. Included in the heading are:

a) taxes levied predominantly on income or profits, though partially on other bases. Taxes on various bases which are not predominantly income or profits are classified according to the principles laid down in §27 and §77;

b) taxes on property, which are levied on a presumed or estimated income as part of an income tax (see also §42(a), (c) and (d));

c) compulsory payments to social security fund contributions that are levied on income but do not confer an entitlement to social benefits. When such contributions do confer an entitlement to social benefits, they are included in heading 2000 (see §34);

d) receipts from integrated scheduler income tax systems are classified as a whole in this heading, even though certain of the scheduler taxes may be based upon gross income and may not take into account the personal circumstances of the taxpayer.

30. The main subdivision of this heading is between levies on individuals (1100) and those on corporate enterprises (1200). Under each subdivision a distinction is made between taxes on income and profits (1110 and 1210), and taxes on capital gains (1120 and 1220). If certain receipts cannot be identified as appropriate to either 1100 or 1200, or if in practice this distinction cannot be made (e.g. because there are no reliable data on the recipients of payments from which withholding taxes are deducted) they are classified in 1300 as not-allocable.

Treatment of credits under imputation systems

31. Under imputation systems of corporate income tax, a company's shareholders are wholly or partly relieved of their liability to income tax on dividends paid by the company out of income or profits liable to corporate income tax. In countries with such systems,[14] part of the tax on the company's profits is available to provide relief against the shareholders' own tax liability. The relief to the shareholder takes the form of a tax credit, the amount of which may be less than, equal to, or more than the shareholder's overall tax liability. If the tax credit exceeds this tax liability the excess may be payable to the shareholder. As this type of tax credit is an integral part of the imputation system of corporate income tax, any payment to the shareholders is treated as a repayment of tax and not as expenditure (compare the treatment of other tax credits described in §20).

32. As the tax credit under imputation systems (even when exceeding tax liability) is to be regarded as a tax provision, the question arises whether it should be deducted from individual income tax receipts (1110) or corporate income tax receipts (1210). In this Report, the full amount of corporate income tax paid is shown under 1210 and no imputed tax is included under 1110. Thus, the full amount of the credit reduces the amount of 1110 whether the credit results in a reduction of personal income tax liability or whether an actual refund is made because the credit exceeds the income tax liability. (Where, however, such tax credits are deducted from corporation tax in respect of dividends paid to corporations the amounts are deducted from the receipts of 1210.)

1120 and 1220 – *Taxes on capital gains*

33. These sub-headings comprise taxes imposed on capital gains, 1120 covering those levied on the gains of individuals and 1220 those levied on the gains of corporate enterprises, where receipts from such taxes can be separately identified. In many countries this is not the case and the receipts from such taxes are then classified with those from the income tax. Heading 1120 also includes taxes on gains from gambling.

2000 – *Social security contributions*

34. Classified here are all compulsory payments that confer an entitlement to receive a (contingent) future social benefit. Such payments are usually earmarked to finance social benefits and are often paid to institutions of general government that provide such benefits. However, such earmarking is not part of the definition of social security contributions and is not required for a tax to be classified here. However, conferment of an entitlement is required for a tax to be classified under this heading. So, levies on income or payroll that are earmarked for social security funds but do not confer an entitlement to benefit are excluded from this heading and shown under personal income taxes (1100) or taxes on payroll and workforce (3000). Taxes on other bases, such

as goods and services, which are earmarked for social security benefits are not shown here but are classified according to their respective bases because they generally confer no entitlement to social security benefits.

35. Contributions for the following types of social security benefits would, *inter alia*, be included: unemployment insurance benefits and supplements, accident, injury and sickness benefits, old-age, disability and survivors' pensions, family allowances, reimbursements for medical and hospital expenses or provision of hospital or medical services. Contributions may be levied on both employees and employers.

36. Contributions may be based on earnings or payroll ('on a payroll basis') or on net income after deductions and exemptions for personal circumstances ('on an income tax basis'), and the revenues from the two bases should be separately identified if possible. However, where contributions to a general social security scheme are on a payroll basis, but the contributions of particular groups (such as the self-employed) cannot be assessed on this basis and net income is used as a proxy for gross earnings, the receipts may still be classified as being on a payroll basis. In principle, this heading excludes voluntary contributions paid to social security schemes. When separately identifiable these are shown in the memorandum item on the financing of social security benefits. In practice, however, they cannot always be separately identified from compulsory contributions, in which case they are included in this heading.

37. Contributions to social insurance schemes which are not institutions of general government and to other types of insurance schemes, provident funds, pension funds, friendly societies or other saving schemes are not considered as social security contributions. Provident funds are arrangements under which the contributions of each employee and of the corresponding employer on his/her behalf are kept in a separate account earning interest and withdrawable under specific circumstances. Pension funds are separately organised schemes negotiated between employees and employers and carry provisions for different contributions and benefits, sometimes more directly tied to salary levels and length of service than under social security schemes. When contributions to these schemes are compulsory or quasi-compulsory (e.g. by virtue of agreement with professional and union organisations) they are shown in the memorandum item (refer to Chapter 4.2 of the Report).

38. Contributions by government employees and by governments in respect of their employees, to social security schemes classified within general government are included in this heading. Contributions to separate schemes for government employees, which can be regarded as replacing general social security schemes, are also regarded as taxes.[15] Where, however, a separate scheme is not seen as replacing a general scheme and has been negotiated between the government, in its role as an employer, and its employees, it is not regarded as social security and contributions to it are not regarded as taxes, even though the scheme may have been established by legislation.

39. This heading excludes 'imputed' contributions, which correspond to social benefits paid directly by employers to their employees or former employees or to their representatives (e.g. when employers are legally obliged to pay sickness benefits for a certain period).

40. Contributions are divided into those of employees (2100), employers (2200), and self-employed or non-employed (2300), and then further sub-divided according to the basis on which they are levied. Employees are defined for this purpose as all persons engaged in activities of business units, government bodies, private non-profit institutions, or other paid employment, except the proprietors and their unpaid family members in the case of unincorporated businesses. Members of the armed forces are included, irrespective of

the duration and type of their service, if they contribute to social security schemes. The contributions of employers are defined as their payments on account of their employees to social security schemes. Where employees or employers are required to continue the payment of social security contributions when the employee becomes unemployed these contributions, data permitting, are shown in 2100 and 2200 respectively. Accordingly, the sub-heading 2300 is confined to contributions paid by the self-employed and by those outside of the labour force (e.g. disabled or retired individuals).

3000 – *Taxes on payroll and workforce*

41. This heading covers taxes paid by employers, employees or the self-employed either as a proportion of payroll or as a fixed amount per person, and which do not confer entitlement to social benefits. Examples of taxes classified here are the United Kingdom national insurance surcharge (introduced in 1977), the Swedish payroll tax (1969–1979), and the Austrian Contribution to the Family Burden Equalisation Fund and Community Tax.

4000 – *Taxes on property*

42. This heading covers recurrent and non-recurrent taxes on the use, ownership or transfer of property. These include taxes on immovable property or net wealth, taxes on the change of ownership of property through inheritance or gift and taxes on financial and capital transactions. The following kinds of tax are excluded from this heading:

a) taxes on capital gains resulting from the sale of a property (1120 or 1220);

b) taxes on the use of goods or on permission to use goods or perform activities (5200); see §72;

c) taxes on immovable property levied on the basis of a presumed net income which take into account the personal circumstances of the taxpayer. They are classified as income taxes along with taxes on income and capital gains derived from property (1100);

d) taxes on the use of property for residence, where the tax is payable by either proprietor or tenant and the amount payable is a function of the user's personal circumstances (pay, dependants, and so on). They are classified as taxes on income (1100);

e) taxes on building in excess of permitted maximum density, taxes on the enlargement, construction or alteration of certain buildings beyond a permitted value and taxes on building construction. They are classified as taxes on permission to perform activities (5200);

f) taxes on the use of one's own property for special trading purposes like selling alcohol, tobacco, meat or for exploitation of land resources (e.g. United States severance taxes). They are classified as taxes on permission to perform activities (5200).

4100 – *Recurrent taxes on immovable property*

43. This sub-heading covers taxes levied regularly in respect of the use or ownership of immovable property.

- these taxes are levied on land and buildings;
- they can be in the form of a percentage of an assessed property value based on a national rental income, sales price, or capitalised yield; or in terms of other characteristics of real property, (for example size or location) from which a presumed rent or capital value can be derived.

- such taxes can be levied on proprietors, tenants, or both. They can also be paid by one level of government to another level of government in respect of property under the jurisdiction of the latter.
- debts are not taken into account in the assessment of these taxes, and they differ from taxes on net wealth in this respect.

44. Taxes on immovable property are further sub-divided into those paid by households (4110) and those paid by other entities (4120), according to the criteria set out in §25*(b)* above.

4200 – *Recurrent taxes on net wealth*

45. This sub-heading covers taxes levied regularly (in most cases annually) on net wealth, i.e. taxes on a wide range of movable and immovable property, net of debt. It is sub-divided into taxes paid by individuals (4210) and taxes paid by corporate enterprises (4220) according to the criteria set out in §25(a) above. If separate figures exist for receipts paid by institutions, the tax payments involved are added to those paid by corporations.

4300 – *Estate, inheritance and gift taxes*

46. This sub-heading is divided into taxes on estates and inheritances (4310) and taxes on gifts (4320).[16] Estate taxes are charged on the amount of the total estate whereas inheritance taxes are charged on the shares of the individual recipients; in addition the latter may take into account the relationship of the individual recipients to the deceased.

4400 – *Taxes on financial and capital transactions*

47. This sub-heading comprises, *inter alia*, taxes on the issue, transfer, purchase and sale of securities, taxes on cheques, and taxes levied on specific legal transactions such as validation of contracts and the sale of immovable property. The heading does not include:

a) taxes on the use of goods or property or permission to perform certain activities (5200);

b) fees paid to cover court charges, charges for birth, marriage or death certificates, which are normally regarded as non-tax revenues (see §9);

c) taxes on capital gains (1000);

d) recurrent taxes on immovable property (4100);

e) recurrent taxes on net wealth (4200);

f) once-and-for-all levies on property or wealth (4500).

4500 – *Other non-recurrent taxes on property*[16]

48. This sub-heading covers once-and-for-all, as distinct from recurrent, levies on property. It is divided into taxes on net wealth (4510) and other non-recurrent taxes on property (4520). Heading 4510 would include taxes levied to meet emergency expenditures, or for redistribution purposes. Heading 4520 would cover taxes levied to take account of increases in land value due to permission given to develop or provision of additional local facilities by general government, any taxes on the revaluation of capital and once-and-for-all taxes on particular items of property.

4600 – *Other recurrent taxes on property*

49. These rarely exist in OECD member countries, but the heading would include taxes on goods such as cattle, jewellery, windows, and other external signs of wealth.

5000 – *Taxes on goods and services*

50. All taxes and duties levied on the production, extraction, sale, transfer, leasing or delivery of goods, and the rendering of services (5100), or in respect of the use of goods or permission to use goods or to perform activities (5200) are included here. The heading thus covers:

a) multi-stage cumulative taxes;

b) general sales taxes – whether levied at manufacture/production, wholesale or retail level;

c) value-added taxes;

d) excises;

e) taxes levied on the import and export of goods;

f) taxes levied in respect of the use of goods and taxes on permission to use goods, or perform certain activities;

g) taxes on the extraction, processing or production of minerals and other products.

51. Borderline cases between this heading and heading 4000 (taxes on property) and 6100 (other taxes on business) are referred to in §42, §47 and §74. Residual sub-headings (5300) and (5130) cover tax receipts which cannot be allocated between 5100 and 5200 and between 5110 and 5120, respectively; see §27.

5100 – *Taxes on the production, sale, transfer, leasing and delivery of goods and rendering of services*

52. This sub-heading consists of all taxes, levied on transactions in goods and services on the basis of their intrinsic characteristics (e.g. value, weight of tobacco, strength of alcohol, and so on) as distinct from taxes imposed on the use of goods, or permission to use goods or perform activities, which fall under 5200.

5110 – *General taxes on goods and services*

53. This sub-heading includes all taxes, other than import and export duties (5123 and 5124), levied on the production, leasing, transfer, delivery or sales of a wide range of goods and/or the rendering of a wide range of services, irrespective of whether they are domestically produced or imported and irrespective of the stage of production or distribution at which they are levied. It thus covers value-added taxes, sales taxes and multi-stage cumulative taxes. Receipts from border adjustments in respect of such taxes when goods are imported are added to gross receipts for this category, and repayments of such taxes when goods are exported are deducted. These taxes are subdivided into 5111 value-added taxes, 5112 sales taxes, 5113 other general taxes on goods and services.

54. Borderline cases arise between this heading and taxes on specific goods (5120) when taxes are levied on a large number of goods, for example, the United Kingdom purchase tax (repealed in 1973) and the Japanese commodity tax (repealed in 1988). In conformity with national views, the former United Kingdom purchase tax is classified as a general tax (5112) and the former Japanese commodity tax as excises (5121).

5111 – *Value-added taxes*

55. All general consumption taxes charged on value-added are classified in this sub-heading, irrespective of the method of deduction and the stages at which the taxes are levied. In practice, all OECD countries with value-added taxes normally allow immediate deduction of taxes on purchases by all but the final consumer and impose

tax at all stages. In some countries the heading may include certain taxes, such as those on financial and insurance activities, either because receipts from them cannot be identified separately from those from the value-added tax, or because they are regarded as an integral part of the value-added tax, even though similar taxes in other countries might be classified elsewhere (e.g. 5126 as taxes on services or 4400 as taxes on financial and capital transactions).

5112 – *Sales taxes*

56. All general taxes levied at one stage only, whether at manufacturing or production, wholesale or retail stage are classified here.

5113 – *Other general taxes on goods and services*

57. This sub-heading covers multi-stage cumulative taxes (also know as 'cascade taxes') where tax is levied each time a transaction takes place without deduction for tax paid on inputs, and also those general consumption taxes where elements of value-added, sales or cascade taxes are combined.

5120 – *Taxes on specific goods and services*

58. Excises, profits generated and transferred from fiscal monopolies, and customs and imports duties as well as taxes on exports, foreign exchange transactions, investment goods and betting stakes and special taxes on services, which do not form part of a general tax of 5110, are included in this category.

5121 – *Excises*

59. Excises are taxes levied on particular products, or on a limited range of products, which are not classifiable under 5110 (general taxes), 5123 (import duties) and 5124 (export duties). They may be imposed at any stage of production or distribution and are usually assessed by reference to the weight or strength or quantity of the product, but sometimes by reference to value. Thus, special taxes on, for example, sugar, beetroot, matches, chocolates, and taxes at varying rates on a certain range of goods, as well as those levied in most countries on tobacco goods, alcoholic drinks and hydrocarbon oils and other energy sources, are included in this sub-heading.

60. Excises are distinguished from:

a) 5110 (general taxes). This is discussed in §53-54;

b) 5123 (import duties). If a tax collected principally on imported goods also applies, or would apply, under the law by which the tax is imposed to comparable home-produced goods, the receipts there from would be classified as excises (5121). This principle applies even if there is no comparable home production or no possibility of it (see also §64);

c) 5126 (taxes on services). The problem here arises in respect of taxes on electricity, gas and energy. All of these are regarded as taxes on goods and are included under 5121.

5122 – *Profits of fiscal monopolies*

61. This sub-heading covers that part of the profits of fiscal monopolies which is transferred to general government or which is used to finance any expenditures considered to be government expenditures (see §18). Amounts are shown when they are transferred to general government or used to make expenditures considered to be government expenditures

62. Fiscal monopolies reflect the exercise of the taxing power of government by the use of monopoly powers. Fiscal monopolies are non-financial public enterprises exercising a monopoly in most cases over the production or distribution of tobacco, alcoholic beverages, salt, matches, playing cards and petroleum or agricultural products (i.e. on the kind of products which are likely to be, alternatively or additionally, subject to the excises of 5121), to raise the government revenues which in other countries are gathered through taxes on dealings in such commodities by private business units. The government monopoly may be at the production stage or, as in the case of government-owned and controlled liquor stores, at the distribution stage.

63. Fiscal monopolies are distinguished from public utilities such as rail transport, electricity, post offices, and other communications, which may enjoy a monopoly or quasi-monopoly position but where the primary purpose is normally to provide basic services rather than to raise revenue for government. Transfers from such other public enterprises to the government are considered as non-tax revenues. The traditional concept of fiscal monopoly is not generally extended to include state lotteries, the profits of which are usually accordingly regarded as non-tax revenues. However, they can be included as tax revenues if the prime reason for their operation is to raise revenues to finance government expenditure. Fiscal monopoly profits are distinguished from export and import monopoly profits (5127) transferred from marketing boards or other enterprises dealing with international trade.

5123 – *Customs and other import duties*

64. Taxes, stamp duties and surcharges restricted by law to imported products are included here. Also included are levies on imported agricultural products which are imposed in member countries of the European Union and amounts paid by certain of these countries under the Monetary Compensation Accounts (MCA) system.[17] Starting from 1998, customs duties collected by European Union member states on behalf of the European Union are no longer reported under this heading in the country tables (in Chapter 4 of the Report). Excluded here are taxes collected on imports as part of a general tax on goods and services, or an excise applicable to both imported and domestically produced goods.

5124 – *Taxes on exports*

65. In the 1970s, export duties were levied in Australia, Canada and Portugal as a regular measure and they have been used in Finland for counter-cyclical purposes. Some member countries of the European Union pay, as part of the MCA system, a levy on exports (see note 16 to §64). Where these amounts are identifiable, they are shown in this heading. This heading does not include repayments of general consumption taxes or excises or customs duties on exported goods, which should be deducted from the gross receipts under 5110, 5121 or 5123, as appropriate.

5125 – *Taxes on investment goods*

66. This sub-heading covers taxes on investment goods, such as machinery. These taxes may be imposed for a number of years or temporarily for counter-cyclical purposes. Taxes on industrial inputs which are also levied on consumers [e.g. the Swedish energy tax which is classified under (5121)] are not included here.

5126 – *Taxes on specific services*

67. All taxes assessed on the payment for specific services, such as taxes on insurance premiums, banking services, gambling and betting stakes (e.g. from horse races, football pools, lottery tickets), transport, entertainment, restaurant and advertising charges, fall into this category. Taxes levied on the gross income of companies providing the service

(e.g. gross insurance premiums or gambling stakes received by the company) are also classified under this heading. Tax revenues from bank levies and payments to deposit insurance and financial stability schemes are provisionally included here for the 2012 edition. The detailed classification is set out in paragraph 104.

68. Excluded from this sub-heading are:

a) taxes on services forming part of a general tax on goods and services (5110);

b) taxes on electricity, gas and energy (5121 as excises);

c) taxes on individual gains from gambling (1120 as taxes on capital gains of individuals and non-corporate enterprises) and lump-sum taxes on the transfer of private lotteries or on the permission to set up lotteries (5200);[18]

d) taxes on cheques and on the issue, transfer or redemption of securities (4400 as taxes on financial and capital transactions).

5127 – *Other taxes on international trade and transactions*

69. This sub-heading covers revenue received by the government from the purchase and sale of foreign exchange at different rates. When the government exercises monopoly powers to extract a margin between the purchase and sales price of foreign exchange, other than to cover administrative costs, the revenue derived constitutes a compulsory levy exacted in indeterminate proportions from both purchaser and seller of foreign exchange. It is the common equivalent of an import duty and export duty levied in a single exchange rate system or of a tax on the sale or purchase of foreign exchange. Like the profits of fiscal monopolies and import or export monopolies transferred to government, it represents the exercise of monopoly powers for tax purposes and is included in tax revenues.

70. The sub-heading covers also the profits of export or import monopolies, which do not however exist in OECD countries, taxes on purchase or sale of foreign exchange, and any other taxes levied specifically on international trade or transactions.

5128 – *Other taxes on specific goods and services*

71. This item includes taxes on the extraction of minerals, fossil fuels and other exhaustible resources from deposits owned privately or by another government together with any other unidentifiable receipts from taxes on specific goods and services. Taxes on the extraction of exhaustible resources are usually a fixed amount per unit of quality or weight, but can be a percentage of value. The taxes are recorded when the resources are extracted. Payments from the extraction of exhaustible resources from deposits owned by the government unit receiving the payment are classified as rent.

5200 – *Taxes on use of goods or on permission to use goods or perform activities*

72. This sub-heading covers taxes which are levied in respect of the use of goods as distinct from taxes on the goods themselves. Unlike the latter taxes – reported under 5100 –, they are not assessed on the value of the goods but usually as fixed amounts. Taxes on permission to use goods or to perform activities are also included here, as are pollution taxes not based upon the value of particular goods. It is sometimes difficult to distinguish between compulsory user charges and licence fees which are regarded as taxes and those which are excluded as non-tax revenues. The criteria which are employed are noted in §9–10.

73. Although the sub-heading refers to the 'use' of goods, registration of ownership rather than use may be what generates liability to tax, so that the taxes of this heading may apply to the ownership of animals or goods rather than their use (e.g. race horses, dogs and motor vehicles) and may apply even to unusable goods (e.g. unusable motor vehicles or guns).

74. Borderline cases arise with:

a) taxes on the permission to perform business activities which are levied on a combined income, payroll or turnover base and, accordingly, are classified following the rules in §77;

b) taxes on the ownership or use of property of headings 4100, 4200 and 4600. The heading 4100 is confined to taxes on the ownership or tenancy of immovable property and – unlike the taxes of 5200 – they are related to the value of the property. The net wealth taxes and taxes on chattels of 4200 and 4600 respectively are confined to the ownership rather than the use of assets, apply to groups of assets rather than particular goods and again are related to the value of the assets.

5210 – *Recurrent taxes on use of goods and on permission to use goods or perform activities*

75. The principal characteristic of taxes classified here is that they are levied at regular intervals and that they are usually fixed amounts. The most important item in terms of revenue receipts is vehicle licence taxes. This sub-heading also covers taxes on permission to hunt, shoot, fish or to sell certain products and taxes on the ownership of dogs and on the performance of certain services, provided that they meet the criteria set out in §9–10. The sub-divisions of 5210 are user taxes on motor vehicles paid by households (5211) and those paid by others (5212).[19] Sub-heading 5213 covers dog licences and user charges for permission to perform activities such as selling meat or liquor when the levies are on a recurring basis. It also covers recurrent general licences for hunting, shooting and fishing where the right to carry out these activities is not granted as part of a normal commercial transaction (e.g. the granting of the licence is not accompanied by the right to use a specific area which is owned by government).

5220 – *Non-recurrent taxes on use of goods and on permission to use goods or perform activities*

76. This section covers non-recurrent taxes levied on the use of goods or on permission to use goods or perform activities and taxes levied each time goods are used. It includes taxes levied on the emission or discharge into the environment of noxious gases, liquids or other harmful substances.

- Payments for tradable emission permits issued by governments under cap and trade schemes should be recorded here at the time the emissions occur. No revenue should be recorded for permits that governments issue free of charge. The accrual basis of recording means that there can be a timing difference between the cash being received by government for the permits and the time the emission occurs. In the national accounts, this timing gives rise to a financial liability for government during the period.
- Payments made for the collection and disposal of waste or noxious substances by public authorities should be excluded as they constitute a sale of services to enterprises.

77. Other taxes falling under heading 5200 that are not levied recurrently are also included here. Thus, once-and-for-all payments for permission to sell liquor or tobacco or to set up betting shops are included provided they meet the criteria set out in §9–10.

6000 – *Other taxes*

78. Taxes levied on a base, or bases, other than those described under headings 1000, 3000, 4000 and 5000, or on bases of which none could be regarded as being predominantly the same as that of any one of these headings, are covered here. As regards taxes levied on a multiple base, if it is possible to estimate receipts related to each base (e.g. the Austrian and German 'Gewerbesteuer') this is done and the separate amounts included under the appropriate headings. If the separate amounts cannot be estimated, but it is

known that most of the receipts are derived from one base, the whole of the receipts are classified according to that base. If neither of these procedures can be followed, they are classified here. The sub-headings may also include receipts from taxes which governments are unable to identify or isolate (see §27). Included here also are fines and penalties paid for infringement of regulations relating to taxes but not identifiable as relating to a particular category of taxes (see §14). A subdivision is made between taxes levied wholly or predominantly on business (6100) and those levied on others (6200).

A.6. Conciliation with National Accounts

79. This section of the tables provides a re-conciliation between the OECD calculation of total tax revenues and the total of all taxes and social contributions paid to general government as recorded in the country's National Accounts. Where the country is a member of the European Union (EU), the comparison is between the OECD calculation of total tax revenues and the sum of tax revenues and social contributions recorded in the combination of the general government and the institutions of the EU sectors of the National Accounts.

A.7. Memorandum item on the financing of social security benefits

80. In view of the varying relationship between taxation and social security contributions and the cases referred to in §34 to §40, a memorandum item collects together all payments earmarked for social security-type benefits, other than voluntary payments to the private sector. Data are presented as follows (refer Chapter 4.2 of the Report):

a) Taxes of 2000 series.

b) Taxes earmarked for social security benefits.

c) Voluntary contributions to the government.

d) Compulsory contributions to the private sector.

Guidance on the breakdown of (a) to (d) above is provided in §34 to §40.

A.8. Memorandum item on identifiable taxes paid by government

81. Identifiable taxes actually paid by government are presented in a memorandum item classified by the main headings of the OECD classification of taxes. In the vast majority of countries, only social security contributions and payroll taxes paid by government can be identified. These are, however, usually the most important taxes paid by governments (refer to Chapter 4.3 of the Report).

A.9. Relation of OECD classification of taxes to national accounting systems

82. A system of national accounts (SNA) seeks to provide a coherent framework for recording and presenting the main flows relating respectively to production, consumption, accumulation and external transactions of a given economic area, usually a country or a major region within a country. Government revenues are an important part of the transactions recorded in SNA. The final version of the 2008 SNA was jointly published by five international organisations: the United Nations, the International Monetary Fund, the European Union, the Organisation for Economic Co-operation and Development, and the World Bank in August 2009. The *System* is a comprehensive, consistent and flexible set of macroeconomic accounts. It is designed for use in countries with market economies, whatever their stage of economic development, and also in countries in transition to market economies. The important parts of the SNA's conceptual framework and its definitions of the various sectors of the economy have been reflected in the OECD's classification of taxes.

83. There are, however, some differences between the OECD classification of taxes and SNA concepts that are listed below. They arise because the aim of the former is to provide the maximum disaggregation of statistical data on what are generally regarded as taxes by tax administrations.

a) OECD includes compulsory social security contributions paid to general government in total tax revenues. Imputed and voluntary contributions plus those paid to private funds are not treated as taxes (§7 and §8 above);

b) there are different points of view on whether or not some levies and fees are classified as taxes (§9 and §10 above);

c) OECD excludes imputed taxes or subsidies resulting from the operation of official multiple exchange rates or from the central bank paying a rate of interest on required reserves that is different from other market rates;

d) there are differences in the treatment of non-wastable tax credits

84. As noted in §1 and §2, headings 1000 to 6000 of the OECD list of taxes cover all unrequited payments to general government, other than compulsory loans and fines. Such unrequited payments including fines, but excluding compulsory loans can be obtained from adding together the following figures in the 2008 SNA

- value-added type taxes (D.211);
- taxes and duties on imports, excluding VAT (D.212);
- export taxes (D.213);
- taxes on products, excluding VAT, import and export taxes (D.214);
- other taxes on production (D.29);
- taxes on income (D.51);
- other current taxes (D.59);
- social contributions (D.61), excluding voluntary contributions;
- capital taxes (D.91).

A.10. The OECD classification of taxes and the International Monetary Fund (GFS) system

85. The coverage and valuation of tax revenues in the GFS system and the 2008 SNA are very similar. Therefore, the differences between the OECD classification and that of the 2008 SNA (see §83 above) also apply to the GFS. In addition the International Monetary Fund subdivides the OECD 5000 heading into section IV (Domestic Taxes on Goods and Services) and section V (Taxes on International Trade and Transactions). This reflects the fact that while the latter usually yield insignificant amounts of revenue in OECD countries, this is not the case in many non-OECD countries.

A.11. Comparison of the OECD classification of taxes with other international classifications

86. The table below describes an item by item comparison of the OECD classification of taxes and the classifications used in the following:

i) System of National Accounts (2008 SNA);

ii) European System of Accounts (1995 ESA);

iii) IMF *Government Finance Statistics Manual* (GFSM2001).

87. These comparisons represent those that would be expected to apply in the majority of cases. However in practice some flexibility should be used in their application. This is because in particular cases, countries can adopt varying approaches to the classification of revenues in National Accounts.

OECD Classification		2008 SNA	2010 ESA	GFSM2014
1000	Taxes on income, profits and capital gains			
	1100 Individuals			
	1110 Income/profits	D51-8.61a	D51A	1111
	1120 Capital gains	D51-8.61c,d	D51C,D	1111
	1200 Corporations			
	1210 Income/profits	D51-8.61b	D51B	1112
	1220 Capital gains	D51-8.61c	D51C	1112
	1300 Unallocable as between 1100 and 1200			1113
2000	Social security contributions			
	2100 Employees	D613-8.85	D613	1211
	2200 Employers	D611-8.83	D611	1212
	2300 Self-employed, non-employed	D613-8.85	D613	1213
	2400 Unallocable as between 2100, 2200 and 2300			1214
3000	Taxes on payroll and workforce	D29-7.97a	D29C	112
4000	Taxes on property			
	4100 Recurrent taxes on immovable property			
	4110 Households	D59-8.63a	D59A	1131
	4120 Other	D29-7.97b	D29A	1131
	4200 Recurrent net wealth taxes			
	4210 Individual	D59-8.63b	D59A	1132
	4220 Corporations	D59-8.63b	D59A	1132
	4300 Estate, inheritance and gift taxes			
	4310 Estate and inheritance taxes	D91-10.207b	D91A	1133
	4320 Gift taxes	D91-10.207b	D91A	1133
	4400 Taxes on financial and capital transactions	D59-7.96d; D29-7.97e	D214B,C	114114; 1161
	4500 Other non-recurrent taxes on property	D91-10.207a	D91B	1135
	4600 Other recurrent taxes on property	D59-8.63c	D59A	1136
5000	Taxes on goods and services			
	5100 Taxes on production, sale and transfer of goods and services			
	5110 General taxes on goods and services			
	5111 Value-added taxes	D211-7.89	D211; D29G	11411
	5112 Sales taxes	D2122-7.94a; D214-7.96a	D21224; D214I	11412
	5113 Other general taxes on goods and services	D214-7.96a	D214I	11413
	5120 Taxes on specific goods and services			
	5121 Excises	D2122-7.94b; D214-7.96b	D21223; D214A,B,D	1142
	5122 Profits of fiscal monopolies	D214-7.96e	D214J	1143
	5123 Customs/import duties	D2121-7.93	D2121; D21221,2	1151
	5124 On exports	D213-7.95a	D214K	1152-4
	5125 On investment goods			
	5126 On specific services	D2122-7.94c; D214-7.96c	D21225; D214E,F,G; D29F	1144; 1156
	5127 Other taxes on international trade and transactions	D2122-7.94d D29-7.95b D29-7.97g D59-8.64d	D21226; D29D; D59E	1153 1155-6
	5128 Other taxes on specific goods and services			1146
	5130 Unallocable as between 5110 and 5120			
	5200 Taxes on use of goods and on permission to use goods or perform activities			
	5210 Recurrent taxes on use of goods and on permission to use goods or perform activities			
	5211 Motor vehicle taxes households	D59-8.64c	D59D	11451
	5212 Motor vehicles taxes others	D29-7.97d	D214D; D29B	11451
	5213 Other recurrent taxes on use of goods and on permission to use goods or perform activities	D29-7.97c,d,f D59-8.64c	D29B,E,F; D59D	11452
	5220 Non-recurrent taxes on permission to use goods or perform activities			
	5300 Unallocable as between 5100 and 5200			
6000	Other taxes			
	6100 Payable solely by business			1161
	6200 Payable by other than business, or unidentifiable	D59-8.64a,b	D59B,C	1162

A.12. Attribution of tax revenues by sub-sectors of general government

88. The OECD classification requires a breakdown of tax revenues by sub-sectors of government. The definition of each sub-sector and the criteria to be used to attribute tax revenues between these sub-sectors are set out below. They follow the guidance of the 2008 SNA and GFSM 2014.

Sub-sectors of general government to be identified

a) Central government

89. The central government sub-sector includes all governmental departments, offices, establishments and other bodies which are agencies or instruments of the central authority whose competence extends over the whole territory, with the exception of the administration of social security funds.Central government therefore has the authority to impose taxes on all resident and non-resident units engaged in economic activities within the country.

b) State, provincial or regional government

90. This sub-sector consists of intermediate units of government exercising a competence at a level below that of central government. It includes all such units operating independently of central government in a part of a country's territory encompassing a number of smaller localities, with the exception of the administration of social security funds. In unitary countries, regional governments may be considered to have a separate existence where they have substantial autonomy to raise a significant proportion of their revenues from sources within their control and their officers are independent of external administrative control in the actual operation of the unit's activities.

91. At present, federal countries comprise the majority of cases where revenues attributed to intermediate units of government are identified separately. Spain is the only unitary country in this position. In the remaining unitary countries, regional revenues are included with those of local governments.

c) Local government

92. This sub-sector includes all other units of government exercising an independent competence in part of the territory of a country, with the exception of the administration of social security funds. It encompasses various urban and/or rural jurisdictions (e.g. local authorities, municipalities, cities, boroughs, districts).

d) Social security funds

93. Social security funds form a separate sub-sector of general government. The social security sub-sector is defined in the 2008 SNA by the following extracts from paragraphs 4.124 to 4.126 and 4.147:

"Social security schemes are social insurance schemes covering the community as a whole or large section of the community that are imposed and controlled by government units. The schemes cover a wide variety of programmes, providing benefits in cash or in kind for old age, invalidity or death, survivors, sickness and maternity, work injury, unemployment, family allowance, health care, etc. There is not necessarily a direct link between the amount of the contribution paid by an individual and the benefits he or she may receive." (Paragraph 4.124).

"When social security schemes are separately organised from the other activities of government units and hold their assets and liabilities separately from the latter and engage in financial transactions on their own account they qualify as institutional units that are described as social security funds." (Paragraph 4.125).

"The amounts raised, and paid out, in social security contributions and benefits may be deliberately varied in order to achieve objectives of government policy that have no direct connection with the concept of social security as a scheme to provide social benefits to members of the community. They may be raised or lowered in order to influence the level of aggregate demand in the economy, for example. Nevertheless, so long as they remain separately constituted funds, they must be treated as separate institutional units in the SNA." (Paragraph 4.126).

"The social security funds sub-sector (of general government) consists of the social security funds operating at all levels of government. Such funds are social insurance schemes covering the community as a whole or large section of the community that are imposed by government units." (Paragraph 4.147).

94. This definition of social security funds is followed in the OECD classification with the two following exceptions which are excluded:

- Schemes imposed by government and operated by bodies outside the general government sector, as defined in §3 of this manual; and
- Schemes to which all contributions are voluntary.

Supra-national authorities

95. This sub-sector covers the revenue-raising operations of supra-national authorities within a country. In practice, the only relevant supra-national authority in the OECD area is that of the institutions of the European Union (EU). As from 1998, supra-national authorities are no longer included in the *Revenue Statistics*, to achieve consistency with the SNA definition of general government which excludes them. For example, income taxes and social security contributions collected by European Institutions and paid by European civil servants who are resident of EU member countries should not be included. However the specific levies paid by the member states of the EU continue to be included in total tax revenues and they are shown under this heading.

Criteria to be used for the attribution of tax revenues

96. When a government collects taxes and pays them over in whole or in part to other governments, it is necessary to determine whether the revenues should be considered to be those of the collecting government which it distributes to others as grants, or those of the beneficiary governments which the collecting government receives and passes on only as their agent. The criteria to be used in the attribution of revenues are set out in §97 to §100 which replicate paragraphs 3.70 to 3.73 from the 2008 SNA

97. In general, a tax is attributed to the government unit that:

a) exercises the authority to impose the tax (either as a principal or through the delegated authority of the principal);

b) has final discretion to set and vary the rate of the tax.

98. Where an amount is collected by one government for and on behalf of another government, and the latter government has the authority to impose the tax, and set and vary its rate, then the former is acting as an agent for the latter and the tax is reassigned. Any amount retained by the collecting government as a collection charge should be treated as a payment for a service. Any other amount retained by the collecting government, such as under a tax-sharing arrangement, should be treated as a current

grant. If the collecting government was delegated the authority to set and vary the rate, then the amount collected should be treated as tax revenue of this government.

99. Where different governments jointly and equally set the rate of a tax and jointly and equally decide on the distribution of the proceeds, with no individual government having ultimate overriding authority, then the tax revenues are attributed to each government according to its respective share of the proceeds. If an arrangement allows one government unit to exercise ultimate overriding authority, then all of the tax revenue is attributed to that unit.

100. There may also be the circumstance where a tax is imposed under the constitutional or other authority of one government, but other governments individually set the tax rate in their jurisdictions. The proceeds of the tax generated in each respective government's jurisdiction are attributed as tax revenues of that government.

Levies paid by member states of the European Union

101. The levies paid by the member states of the EU take the form of special levies which include:

a) custom duties and levies on agricultural goods (5123);

b) gross monetary compensation accounts (5123 if relating to imports and 5124 if relating to exports); and

c) Steel, coal, sugar and milk levies (5128).

102. The custom duties collected by member states on behalf of the EU are recorded:

- on a gross of collection fee basis;
- using figures adjusted so that duties are shown on a 'final destination' as opposed to a 'country of first entry' basis where such adjustments can be made. These adjustments concern in particular duties collected at important (sea) ports. Although the EU duties are collected by the authorities of the country of first entry, when possible these duties should be excluded from the revenue of the collecting country and be included in the revenue of the country of final destination.

103. This is the specific EU levy that most clearly conforms to the attribution criterion described in §95 above. Consequently as from 1998, these amounts are footnoted as a memorandum item to the EU member state country tables (in Chapter 4) and no longer shown under heading 5123. However the figures are included in the total tax revenue figures on the top line for all the relevant years shown in the tables.

A.13. Provisional classification of revenues from bank levies and payments to deposit insurance and financial stability schemes

104. The OECD have adopted the following interim approach to reporting revenue from bank levies plus deposit insurance and stability fees for the 2012 and subsequent editions of *OECD Revenue Statistics*. It is recommended that the amounts should be recorded under category 5126.

- Compulsory payments of stability fees, bank levies and deposit insurance should generally be treated as tax revenues where the payments are made to General Government and allocated to the governments' consolidated or general funds so that the Government is free to make immediate use of the money for the purposes that it chooses. This principle would apply regardless of whether the Government is promising to make payments to guarantee the banks' customer deposits in some future contingency.

- If the compulsory payments are made to general government and placed in funds that are earmarked to be entirely channelled back to the sector of the economy that comprises the companies that are subject to the payment, they would still generally be treated as tax revenues on the grounds that the funds would be available for the government and would reduce its budget deficit, the fee is unrequited for an individual entity and the amounts raised could be unrelated to any eventual pay out to depositors or expenditure on wider support for the financial sector.
- Payments to made to the smaller long-standing schemes for insuring 'retail' deposits, where the payment levels are consistent with the costs of insurance should be classified as fee for service.
- Any payments which involve governments realising the assets of a failed institution or receiving a priority claim on its assets in liquidation in order to fund payments of compensation to customers for their lost deposits would be treated as a fee for a service as opposed to tax revenues.
- Compulsory payments that are made to funds operated outside the government sector and non-state institutions backed by the deposit takers and all payments to voluntary schemes should not be treated as tax revenues.

Notes

1. References in this OECD Interpretative Guide to Sections or Parts of "this Report" refer to OECD (2016a), *Revenue Statistics 2016*, OECD Publishing, Paris.
2. All references to SNA are to the 2008 edition.
3. See section A.12 of this guide for a discussion of the concept of agency capacity.
4. It is usually possible to identify amounts of social security contributions and payroll taxes, but not other taxes paid by government.
5. If, however, a levy which is considered as non-tax revenue by most countries is regarded as a tax – or raises substantial revenue – in one or more countries, the amounts collected are footnoted at the end of the relevant country tables, even though the amounts are not included in total tax revenues.
6. Names, however, can frequently be misleading. For example, though a passport fee would normally be considered a non-tax revenue, if a supplementary levy on passports (as is the case in Portugal) were imposed in order to raise substantial amounts of revenue relative to the cost of providing the passport, the levy would be regarded as a tax under 5200.
7. A more detailed explanation of this distinction can be found in the special feature, "Current issues in reporting tax revenues", in the 2001 edition of the *Revenue Statistics.*
8. Sometimes the terms "non-refundable" and "refundable" are used, but it may be considered illogical to talk of "refundable" when nothing has been paid.
9. A different treatment, however, is accorded to non-wastable tax credits under imputation systems of corporate income tax (§31–33).
10. This is not strictly a true tax expenditure in the formal sense. Such tax expenditures require identification of a benchmark tax system for each country or, preferably, a common international benchmark. In practice it has not been possible to reach agreement on a common international benchmark.
11. Unless based on the profit made on a sale, in which case they would be classified as capital gains taxes under 1120 or 1220.
12. In some countries the same legislation applies to both individual and corporate enterprises for particular taxes on income. However, the receipts from such taxes are usually allocable between individuals and enterprises and can therefore be shown in the appropriate sub-heading.
13. For example, "...sufficiently self-contained and independent that they behave in the same way as corporations.......(including) keeping a complete set of accounts" (2008 SNA, section 4.44).
14. In Canada – a country also referred to as having an imputation system – the (wastable) tax credit for the shareholder is in respect of domestic corporation tax deemed to have been paid whether or not a corporation tax liability has arisen. As there is no integral connection between the corporation tax liability and the credit given against income tax under such systems, these credits for dividends are treated, along with other tax credits, on the lines described in §20.
15. This may also apply where a scheme for government employees existed prior to the introduction of a general social security scheme.
16. In the 2008 SNA these are regarded as capital transfers and not as taxes (see section A.8).
17. This is the system by which the European Union adjusts for differences between the exchange rates used to determine prices under the Common Market Agricultural Policy and actual exchange rates. Payments under the system may relate to imports or exports and where these amounts are separately identifiable they are shown under the appropriate heading (5123 or 5124). In this Report, these amounts are shown gross (i.e. without deducting any subsidies paid out under the MCA system).
18. Transfers of profits of State lotteries are regarded as non-tax revenues (see also §63).
19. See §25(c) as regards this distinction.

ORGANISATION FOR ECONOMIC CO-OPERATION AND DEVELOPMENT

The OECD is a unique forum where governments work together to address the economic, social and environmental challenges of globalisation. The OECD is also at the forefront of efforts to understand and to help governments respond to new developments and concerns, such as corporate governance, the information economy and the challenges of an ageing population. The Organisation provides a setting where governments can compare policy experiences, seek answers to common problems, identify good practice and work to co-ordinate domestic and international policies.

The OECD member countries are: Australia, Austria, Belgium, Canada, Chile, the Czech Republic, Denmark, Estonia, Finland, France, Germany, Greece, Hungary, Iceland, Ireland, Israel, Italy, Japan, Korea, Latvia, Luxembourg, Mexico, the Netherlands, New Zealand, Norway, Poland, Portugal, the Slovak Republic, Slovenia, Spain, Sweden, Switzerland, Turkey, the United Kingdom and the United States. The European Union takes part in the work of the OECD.

OECD Publishing disseminates widely the results of the Organisation's statistics gathering and research on economic, social and environmental issues, as well as the conventions, guidelines and standards agreed by its members.

CENTRE FOR TAX POLICY AND ADMINISTRATION

The Centre for Tax Policy and Administration (CTPA) is the focal point for the OECD's work on taxation. The Centre provides technical expertise and support to the Committee on Fiscal Affairs and examines all aspects of taxation other than macro-fiscal policy. Its work covers international and domestic tax issues, direct and indirect taxes, tax policy and tax administration. CTPA also carries out an extensive global programme of dialogue between OECD and non-OECD tax officials through events held annually on the full range of OECD work, bringing together over 100 non-OECD economies. For information on the Centre for Tax Policy and Administration, please visit *www.oecd.org/tax*.

OECD DEVELOPMENT CENTRE

The OECD Development Centre was established in 1962 as an independent platform for knowledge sharing and policy dialogue between OECD member countries and developing economies, allowing these countries to interact on an equal footing. Today, 27 OECD countries and 24 non-OECD countries are members of the Centre. The Centre draws attention to emerging systemic issues likely to have an impact on global development and more specific development challenges faced by today's developing and emerging economies. It uses evidence-based analysis and strategic partnerships to help countries formulate innovative policy solutions to the global challenges of development.

For more information on the Centre, please see *www.oecd.org/dev*.

OECD PUBLISHING, 2, rue André-Pascal, 75775 PARIS CEDEX 16
(23 2016 42 1 P) ISBN 978-92-64-26647-6 – 2016

www.ingramcontent.com/pod-product-compliance
Lightning Source LLC
LaVergne TN
LVHW081419110826
845149LV00010B/1794

* 9 7 8 9 2 6 4 2 6 6 4 7 6 *